Off-Hand Sketches
A Companion For The Tourist And Traveller Over The Philadelphia, Pottsville, And Reading Railroad

Wm. J. Bromwell

Alpha Editions

This Edition Published in 2021

ISBN: 9789354506222

Design and Setting By
Alpha Editions
www.alphaedis.com
Email – info@alphaedis.com

As per information held with us this book is in Public Domain.
This book is a reproduction of an important historical work. Alpha Editions uses the best technology to reproduce historical work in the same manner it was first published to preserve its original nature. Any marks or number seen are left intentionally to preserve its true form.

OFF-HAND SKETCHES;

A

COMPANION FOR THE TOURIST AND TRAVELLER

OVER THE

PHILADELPHIA, POTTSVILLE, AND READING RAILROAD.

DESCRIBING

THE SCENERY, IMPROVEMENTS, MINERAL AND AGRICULTURAL
RESOURCES, HISTORICAL INCIDENTS, AND OTHER SUBJECTS
OF INTEREST IN THE VICINITY OF THE ROUTE.

With Numerous Engravings.

PHILADELPHIA:
PUBLISHED BY J. W. MOORE,
195 CHESTNUT STREET.
1854.

TABLE OF DISTANCES BETWEEN

Philadelphia and Cincinnati,

VIA RAILROAD.

PENNSYLVANIA RAILROAD.—PASSENGER STATIONS, 1853.

Miles.		Dist. Betw. Stat's.	Miles.		Dist. Betw. Stat's.	Miles.		Dist. Betw. Stat's.
	PHILADELPHIA,		121	Aqueduct,	3	248	Plane No. 8	2
4	Hestonville,	4	127	Baily's,	6	252	Summit,	4
9	White Hall,	5	131	Newport,	4	255	Plane No. 4,	3
13	Morgan's Corner,	4	137	Millerstown,	6	258	Plane No. 2,	3
15	Eagle,	2	142	Thompsontown,	5	262	Jefferson,	4
20	Paoli,	5	148	Mexico,	6	266	Half-Way House,	4
25	Steamboat	5	150	Perryville,	2	269	Viaduct,	3
29	Oakland,	4	153	Mifflin,	3	275	Conemaugh,	6
32	Downingtown,	3	165	LEWISTOWN,	12	277	JOHNSTOWN,	2
33	Gallagherville,	1	173	Anderson,	7	282	Nineveh,	9
38	Coatsville,	5	177	McVeytown,	5	290	Florence,	4
43	Parksburg,	5	182	Manayunk,	5	295	Lockport,	5
46	Penningtonville,	3	187	Newton Hamilton,	5	297	Bolivar,	2
50	Gap,	4	190	Mount Union	3	302	Blairsville Intersect'n,	5
53	Kinzer's,	3	193	Mapleton,	3		Blairsville,	
56	Lemonplace,	3	196	Mill Creek,	3	306	Hillside,	4
61	Bird in Hand,	5	201	HUNTINGDON,	5	310	Derry,	4
68	LANCASTER,	7	208	Petersburgh,	7	315	Latrobe,	5
69	Dillerville,	1	211	Barree,	3	317	BEATY'S	2
74	Landisville,	5	214	Spruce Creek,	3	324	Greensburg,	7
80	Mount Joy,	6	218	Birmingham,	4	327	Radebaugh's,	3
86	Elizabethtown,	6	221	Tyrone,	3	332	Manor,,	5
95	Middleton,	9	225	Tipton's	4	334	Irwin's	2
98	Highspire,	3	227	Fostoria,	2	339	Stewart's,	5
104	HARRISBURGH,	6	229	Bell's Mill,	2	344	Brinton's,	5
109	Rockville,	5	235	Altoona,	6	349	Wilkinsburgh,	5
114	Cove,	5	242	HOLLIDAYSBURGH INT.,	7	351	Liberty,	2
118	Duncannon,	4	246	Plane No. 9,	4	355	PITTSBURGH,	4

PASSENGERS CHANGE BAGGAGE CHECKS.

OHIO AND PENNSYLVANIA RAILROAD.

Miles.		Dist. Betw. Stat's.	Miles.		Dist. Betw. Stat's.	Miles.		Dist. Betw. Stat's.
361	Courtney's,	5	449	Louisville,	6	552	Iberia,	7
365	Haysville,	4	455	Canton,	6	559	Gilead,	7
376	Sewickley,	2	463	MASSILLON,	8	565	Cardington,	6
369	Shousetown,	2	470	Lawrence,	7	571	Oxford,	7
372	Economy,	3	474	Fairview,	4	579	Delaware,	8
375	Baden,	3	478	Orrville,	4	586	Orange,	7
378	Freedom,	3	481	Paradise,	3	572	Worthington,	6
380	Rochester,	2	489	WOOSTER,	8	602	COLUMBUS,	10
383	New Brighton,	3	495	Millbrook,	6	616	West Jefferson,	14
393	Darlington,	10	499	Clinton,	4	627	Loudon,	11
399	Enon,	6	505	Lakeville,	6	643	Selma,	16
402	Palestine,	5	510	Loudonville,	5	649	Cedarville,	6
409	Bull Creek,	5	516	Perryville,	6	657	XENIA,	8
414	Columbiana,	5	522	Lucas,	6	664	Spring Valley,	7
420	Franklin,	6	527	MANSFIELD,	5	671	Corwin,	7
424	Salem,	4	534	Spring Mill,	7	677	Oregon,	6
429	Damascus,	5	542	CRESTLINE,	8	690	Deerfield,	13
432	Smithfield	3				705	Miamiville,	15
437	ALLIANCE,	5	CLEVE. COL. & CIN. RAIL ROAD.			712	Plainville,	7
443	Strasburg,	6	545	Galion,	3	722	CINCINNATI,	10

Philadelphia and Reading Railroad.

PASSENGER TRAIN TIME TABLE.

Leave Philadelphia from the Depot, Broad and Callowhill Street, at 7¼ A. M., and 3½ P. M. Daily Except Sundays, when an Excursion Train leaves at 7½ A. M. Returning leaves Pottsville at 4 P. M.

UP TRAINS.			DOWN TRAINS.		
STATIONS.	Exp's Morn.	Way Aft'n.	STATIONS.	Wag Morn.	Exp's Aft'n.
Leaves PHILADELPHIA,	7.30	3.30	Leaves POTTSVILLE,	7.30	3.30
Passes Schl. Viaduct,	—	3.41	Passes MT. CARBON,	7.37	3.37
" Manayunk,	—	3.50	" SCHL. HAVEN,	7.46	3.45
" Conshohocken,	—	4.05	" Orwigsburg,	7.57	—
" Norristown,	—	4.12	" Auburn,	8.05	—
" Port Kennedy,	—	4.21	" PORT CLINTON,	8.20	4.10
" Valley Forge,	—	4.26	" Hamburg,	8.30	—
" PHŒNIXVILLE,	8.31	4.41	" Mohrsville,	8.48	—
" Royer's Ford,	—	4.51	" Althouse's,	8.53	—
" Limerick,	—	4.56	" READING,	9.10	4.51
" POTTSTOWN,	8.58	5.13	" Birdsboro,	9.32	—
" Douglassville,	—	5.22	" Douglassville,	9.41	—
" Birdsboro,	—	5.33	" POTTSTOWN,	9.51	5.30
" READING,	9.34	6.00	" Limerick,	10.04	—
" Althouse's,	—	6.25	" Royer's Ford,	10.08	—
" Mohrsville,	—	6.30	" PHŒNIXVILLE,	10.18	5.56
" Hamburg,	—	6.48	" Valley Forge,	10.29	—
" PORT CLINTON,	10.17	6.58	" Port Kennedy,	10.34	—
" Auburn,	—	7.11	" Norristown,	10.44	—
" Orwigsburg,	—	7.19	" Conshohocken,	10.51	—
" SCHL. HAVEN,	10.43	7.27	" Manayunk,	11.06	—
" MOUNT CARBON,	10.52	7.36	" Schl. Viaduct,	11.18	—
Arrives at POTTSVILLE,	11.00	7.45	Arrives at PHILAD'A.	11.30	7.00

STAGE CONNEXIONS.

At PHŒNIXVILLE, with Express and Way Trains, for Yellow Springs, &c.
At POTTSTOWN, with Express Trains, for Boyerstown, Allentown, &c.
At READING, with Express Trains, for Lebanon, Harrisburg, Bernville, Jonestown, &c.
At POTTSVILLE, with Express Trains, for Northumberland, Sunbury, Danville, Catawissa, &c.

RAILROAD CONNEXIONS.

At PORT CLINTON, to Tamaqua, thence by Stage to Mauch Chunk, Wilkesbarre, Lackawanna, Hazelton, &c.
At SCHUYLKILL HAVEN, to Minersville, Tremont, &c.
At MOUNT CARBON, to Tuscarora, Middleport, &c.

Philadelphia and Reading Railroad.

PASSENGER FARES AND DISTANCES.

UP TRAINS.				DOWN TRAINS.			
Dist.	From Philad'a to	FARES. No. 1	No. 2	Dist.	From Pottsville to	FARES. No. 1	No. 2
3½	Schl. Viaduct,	.15	.10	1	Mount Carbon,	.05	.05
7	Manayunk,	.20	.15	4	Schl. Haven,	.15	.10
13½	Conshohocken,	.30	.25	7	Orwigsburg,	.20	.15
17	Norristown,	.40	.30	10	Auburn,	.30	.25
21½	Port Kennedy,	.65	.50	15	Port Clinton,	.45	.35
23½	Valley Forge,	.70	.60	18	Hamburg,	.55	.45
27½	Phœnixville,	.80	.65	25	Mohrsville,	.75	.60
32	Royer's Ford,	.95	.80	27	Althouse's,	.80	.65
34	Limerick,	1.05	.85	35	Reading,	1.05	.85
40	Pottstown,	1.20	1.00	44	Birdsboro,	1.30	1.10
44½	Douglassville,	1.35	1.10	48½	Douglassville,	1.45	1.20
49	Birdsboro,	1.50	1.25	53	Pottstown,	1.60	1.30
58	Reading,	1.75	1.45	59	Limerick,	1.75	1.45
66	Althouse's,	2.00	1.65	61	Royer's Ford,	1.80	1.50
68	Mohrsville,	2.05	1.70	65½	Phœnixville,	1.95	1.65
75	Hamburg,	2.25	1.90	69½	Valley Forge,	2.05	1.70
78	Port Clinton,	2.35	1.95	71½	Port Kennedy,	2.10	1.75
83	Auburn,	2.50	2.10	76	Norristown,	2.35	1.95
86	Orwigsburg,	2.60	2.15	79½	Conshohocken,	2.45	2 00
89	Schl. Haven,	2.70	2.20	86	Manayunk,	2.55	2.15
92	Mount Carbon,	2.75	2.25	89½	Schl. Viaduct.	2.65	2.20
93	Pottsville,	2.75	2.25	93	Philadelphia.	2.75	2.25

Way Trains stop at all the points stated: Express Trains only at those Stations in Small Capitals, and *positively* at no others.

All Passengers will purchase their tickets before entering the cars.

Fifty pounds of Baggage are allowed each Passenger.

Passengers are strictly forbidden to stand outside, on the Platforms, while the cars are in motion.

Passengers waiting for Way Trains, at Way Points where there is no Railroad Agent, will signal the approaching Trains, otherwise they will not stop.

A WORD BEFORE WE GO.

In all parts of Europe the traveller is supplied with Guide-books, detailing, for his special information and satisfaction, the leading features of all objects of interest on his route. There is not an antiquated castle, a battle-field, a mountain, or a river, but has its peculiar points revealed for the entertainment of the stranger, as he rambles along from place to place. No doubt this materially adds to the interest and subsequent *value* of travel; and probably constitutes one of the paramount attractions of a tour in Europe, since all its incidents are thus permanently impressed on the mind.

In the United States no such conveniences exist; and this is probably one reason why foreigners generally misunderstand and misrepresent us —they are not *sufficiently informed* to give a correct estimate of our resources, peculiarities, and institutions. They hastily pass over our railways and rivers, and, for the want of suitable printed-guides, return as profoundly ignorant of the routes traversed as they were at the starting-point—for seeing is not *understanding*.

In her physical aspect and resources, Pennsylvania is pre-eminently the most interesting State in the Union—yet, for the want of *popular descriptions* and references, her real character is comparatively obscured from the public view. The most intelligent individual may make the tour from the Delaware to the Ohio by railroad, and yet be unable to identify one-half the towns, or mountains, or streams, or otherwise explain correctly the prominent local characteristics of the route traversed. Thousands of persons, of fortune and leisure, owing to this evil, are intimidated from travelling; while many proceed direct to Europe, before visiting the objects of interest in their own immediate land.

It was as much with the hope of converting our time to a useful purpose, as receiving a reasonable compensation for it, that we undertook to sketch, in a sprightly and popular way, some of the prominent features of our time-honoured Commonwealth. If we have collected together, in tolerable order, a mass of matter that will relieve, to some extent, the fatigue and monotony of travel, our main object has been attained.

We may add, that over seventeen hundred dollars have been expended for pictorial illustrations, some of which we can point to as fair specimens of the art. During the particular time we were engaged in the preparation of these pages, however, an unusual activity prevailed among our best wood engravers, in consequence of large orders from the Government. We were, therefore, in several instances, forced to employ artists of ordinary talent—though, upon the whole, we think the reader will find little to complain of under this head.

The matter is, what it purports to be, off-hand, and no particular credit is claimed or expected for it. We have profited from the works of others to a greater extent than we should, had our time been less limited. Our acknowledgments are due to the works of the late Prof. Richardson, and to those of Mr. Day, Mr. Trego, and others, from which the matter not strictly original has been mainly extracted. With these explanations our work is done.

E. B.

N. B.—It is proper to add, that not having corrected the latter portion of this work as it was passing through the press, some errors appear which would not otherwise have occurred.

PENNSYLVANIA.

BY PHILIP FRENEAU.

Spread with stupendous hills, far from the main,
Fair Pennsylvania holds her golden reign;
In fertile fields her wheaten harvest grows,
Charged with its freights her favorite *Delaware* flows;
From Erie's lake her soil with plenty teems
To where the *Schuylkill* rolls his limpid streams—
Sweet stream! what pencil can thy beauties tell—
Where, wandering downward through the woody vale,
Thy varying scenes to rural bliss invite,
To health and pleasure add a new delight.
Here *Juniata*, too, allures the swain,
And gay *Cadorus* roves along the plain;
Swatara, tumbling from the distant hill,
Steals through the waste, to turn the industrious mill—
Where'er those floods through groves or mountain stray,
That God of nature still directs the way;
With fondest care has traced each river's bed,
And mighty streams thro' mighty forests led;
Bade agriculture thus export her freight,
The strength and glory of this favored State.

   She, famed for science, arts, and polished men,
Admires her Franklin, but adores her Penn,

Who wandering here, made barren forests bloom,
And the new soil a happier robe assume:
He planned no schemes that virtue disapproves,
He robbed no Indian of his native groves,
But, just to all, beheld his tribes increase,
Did what he could to bind the world in peace,
And, far retreating from a selfish band,
Bade Freedom flourish in this foreign land.

Gay towns unnumbered shine through all her plains,
Here every art its happiest height attains:
The graceful ship, on nice proportions planned,
Here finds perfection from the builder's hand,
To distant worlds commercial visits pays,
Or war's bold thunder o'er the deep conveys.

OFF-HAND SKETCHES.

PART I.

The Valley of the Schuylkill.

Let us, since life can little else supply,
Than just to look around us, and to die,
Expatiate free o'er all this scene of man—
A mighty maze, but not without a plan;
A wild, where weeds and flowers promiscuous shoot,
Or garden, tempting with forbidden fruit.
Together let us roam this ample field—
Try what the open, what the covert yield:
Eye Nature's walks—shoot folly as it flies,
And catch the manners, living, as they rise;
Laugh where we must—be candid where we can,
But always vindicate the ways of God to man!

ROM Philadelphia to Pottsville, Tamaqua and Mauch Chunk, thence to Wilkesbarre, in Wyoming:—this is the journey before us. Having seated ourselves in the comfortable cars of the Reading Railroad Company, the first object which arrests our attention, after leaving the depot at Broad near Callowhill street, is the Preston Retreat, a fine marble building on our right; we then catch glimpses of the Eastern Penitentiary, which served as a model for European Institutions of a like character, and of Girard College, the finest building of the kind in the United States, and one of the finest in the world.

GIRARD COLLEGE.

Shortly after which we see, on our left, the Fairmount Water-works, and although a notice of it is not strictly within the range of this work, it may nevertheless prove interesting to many to learn something of its leading features, especially as it was the first establishment of the kind ever erected in the United States; and, in point of boldness of conception and romantic profile, probably inferior to none in any quarter of the globe.

The first water-works were commenced in 1799. A steam-engine was placed in Chestnut street, near the Schuylkill, by means of which the water was elevated to a basin in Penn square, and from thence distributed to the city in wooden pipes. The quantity of water thus obtained was soon found to be entirely too small to supply the increasing demand, and the works were abandoned in 1815, after nearly $700,000 had been spent upon them. In 1816 the works at Fairmount were commenced, the water being again raised by steam to an elevated reservoir. Steam was found too expensive, and arrangements were adopted in 1818, by which the water-power of the river was applied. A dam was erected in a diagonal course across the river, securing a head of water nearly thirty feet in depth, and conducted to the mill-houses, on the eastern side of the stream, as represented in the engraving on the opposite page. Here the water

FAIRMOUNT WATER-WORKS.

is forced up to the reservoir, elevated about one hundred feet above the level of the river, and fifty feet above the highest ground in the city. The reservoir, when full, contains twelve feet of water, and is capable of holding over twenty-two millions of gallons. There are eighty-three miles of water-pipe laid down in the city, exclusive of the works of Spring Garden and the Northern Liberties, which probably have an equal extent in the adjoining districts of the city proper. The daily average consumption of water, from these works, is nearly five million gallons. Their total cost was $1,615,169, and they were designed and executed by the late Frederick Graff, to whose memory a handsome monument is erected in the grounds fronting on the Schuylkill, from a design by his son.

The comparison between the present works and the old steam-works, is greatly to the advantage of the former. It was not possible, with the steam-engines, to raise one million two hundred and fifty thousand gallons per day—whereas, the present works, with only three wheels, can readily raise three times this amount, without any increase of expense. But if the same quantity were required to be raised by additional steam-engines, the annual expense would probably be at least $75,000. In other words, the expense of raising three hundred and seventy-five thousand gallons per day, by steam, would be $206—by water, it is only $4. In this estimate, the first cost of the steam-engines or of the water-power is not considered.

These works are eminently worth a visit from the stranger. They are delightfully situated, and present a view, in connection with surrounding objects, of rare beauty and spirit. The wire-bridge, stretching across the Schuylkill, is also an interesting object, and is probably one of the most complete structures of the kind, as we believe it was one of the first, ever erected in the United States. The accompanying sketch exhibits a faithful view of the Water-works and Wire-bridge, as seen from the opposite side of the river.

Within the suburbs of the city, scattered along the rail-road, several "lager beer" establishments will be noticed. These breweries are all of very recent origin, and lager beer is, to many, an unknown beverage. It is a German drink, of which they are very fond, and is similar in taste and appearance to porter, but is said to have none of its deleterious qualities. It is a weak, bitter, but not unpleasant beer, containing an abundance of hops. It derives its peculiar value and flavor from storage in vaults, as the word "lager" sufficiently implies. The longer it is stored, the finer becomes its quality. The vicinity of Fairmount has lately become the fountain-head of this description of manufacture, and it is consequently a favorite resort for Germans, who, ranged around their little square tables, with cigars, pipes, newspapers and glass-mugs of *lager*,

> Mingle o'er their friendly bowl,
> The feast of reason and the flow of soul.

As we pass Fairmount, the river Schuylkill, with its green banks, soft verdure, and rich foliage, is brought into view—the rail-road, until it crosses the bridge, diverging along its eastern bank. Here a number of spacious warehouses will be noticed, built directly along the water's edge, and affording access for carts by means of scaffolding erected to their upper stories. These are *ice-houses*. They are built with much care, the walls filled in with tan-bark to exclude the air, and capable of storing an immense quantity of ice. The manner of collecting and storing the ice is very simple, and is fully illustrated in the accompanying engraving.

Of late years, the storage and shipment of ice has become a very considerable item of trade. A large quantity is required for the consumption of the city, but in addition to this, no inconsiderable amount is shipped to the South, as well as to foreign countries where the climate forbids its production. Vessels freighted with ice always obtain a return load, and thereby a judicious exchange of local commodities is effected with points where, under other circumstances, our trade would probably be less extensive, and our communication

CUTTING ICE ON THE SCHUYLKILL.

less frequent. Our eastern neighbors, always the first in the market with their "notions," have now a serious competitor in Philadelphia in this branch of commerce.

In seasons of scarcity, ice is brought down the Schuylkill, in the spring, from the mountain regions of Schuylkill county, where, the climate being somewhat colder, and the streams less impregnated with sediment, it attains a good thickness, as well as a pure and transparent quality. On the Schuylkill, it usually attains a thickness of from four to twelve or more inches, and is probably unrivalled for the purity of its mineral composition, and freedom from foreign and deleterious substances. Its color varies from snowy opaqueness to translucency, and sometimes to the most beautiful watery transparency.

As we pass over the splendid rail-road bridge, a very interesting object presents itself. A beautiful little island, overgrown with tall and slender trees, nestles in the midst of the river, and immediately in front of it, on the western shore, is situated an unique cottage, built of stone, and apparently of some antiquity. In front of the cottage are two old trees, wrinkled and gnarled, like the furrows in an old man's face. This cottage is now a rough and dilapidated affair, but it was once the temporary residence of the late Thomas Moore, the celebrated Irish poet. It bears the rather unpoetic name of "Pig's Eye," but to many is known as Tom Moore's cottage. We entered the house while our friend Brightly was sketching it, and found it indeed a relic of the past. The ceilings, which have never been plastered, reveal the rough joists, now blackened with smoke and greasy rust, while the occupants complained of the condition of the roof, which leaks badly. The cottage appeared otherwise warm and comfortable, as answering the humble pretensions of the lessee. But we thought there was some reason for his complaint against the landlord, who failed to put it in tenantable order, after receiving two months' rent in advance. If properly fitted up, it might still serve as the abode of the muse,—but, alas! it can never again return to the scenes of its former glory. It is about forty-five years since Mr. Moore visited this country; and the changes which have been made during this time, are probably no less striking elsewhere than on this spot. At that time, this little cot was surrounded with a comparative wilderness, the abode of merry warblers and of wild-flowers;—the Schuylkill yet flowed in undisturbed tranquillity, and its peaceful shores were fragrant with the rich profusion of its foliage. It was a spot well calculated to tempt the poet from the noisy scenes of the town, and no less calculated to lend inspiration to the harp which has given such celebrity to his melodies.

"I went to America," (says the poet, after his return to Europe,) "with prepossessions by no means unfavorable, and indeed rather indulged in many of those illusive ideas with respect to the purity of the government and the primitive happiness of the people, which I had early imbibed in my native country, where, unfortunately, discontent at home enhances every distant temptation, and the western world has long been looked to as a retreat for real or imaginary oppression; as, in short, the Elysian Atlantis, where persecuted patriots might find their visions realized, and be welcomed by kindred spirits to liberty and repose. In all these flattering expectations I found myself completely disappointed, and felt inclined to say to America, as Horace says to his mistress, "*intentata nites.*" Brissot, in the preface to his travels, observes that 'freedom in that country is carried to so high a degree as to border upon a state of nature;' and there certainly is a close approximation to savage life, not only in the liberty which they enjoy, but in the violence of party spirit, and of private animosity which results from it. . . . . . The rude familiarity of the lower orders, and indeed the unpolished state of society in general, would neither surprise nor disgust if they seemed to flow from that simplicity of character, that honest ignorance of the gloss of refinement, which may be looked for in a new and inexperienced people. But, when we find them arrived at maturity in most of the vices, and all the pride of civilization, while they are still so far removed from its higher and

TOM MOORE'S COTTAGE.

better characteristics, it is impossible not to feel that this youthful decay, this crude anticipation of the natural period of corruption, must repress every sanguine hope of the future energy and greatness of America."

During his brief sojourn on the green banks of the Schuylkill, the poet produced several choice effusions; but it is to be regretted that these gems are associated with so much that, for his own high reputation, had better been "left unsung." In his poem addressed to the Hon. W. R. Spencer, he speaks thus disparagingly of us:

> All that creation's varying mass assumes
> Of grand or lovely, here aspires and blooms;
> Bold rise the mountains, rich the gardens glow,
> Bright lakes expand, and conquering rivers flow;
> But mind, immortal mind, without whose ray
> This world's a wilderness and man but clay;
> Mind, mind alone in barren, still repose,
> Nor blooms, nor rises, nor expands, nor flows.
> Take Christians, Mohawks, Democrats, and all—
> From the rude wigwam to the Congress hall—
> From man the savage—whether slaved or free,—
> To man the civilized, less tame than he,—
> 'Tis one dull chaos, one unfertile strife
> Betwixt half-polished, and half-barbarous life;
> Where every ill the ancient world could brew
> Is mixed with every grossness of the new,—
> Where all corrupts, though little can entice,
> And naught is known of luxury but its vice.

In his sweeping denunciations of the American character, he spares only the "sacred few" whom he met in Philadelphia:

> Yet, yet forgive me, oh ye sacred few,
> Whom late by Delaware's green banks I knew;
> Whom, known and loved through many a social eve,
> 'Twas bliss to live with, and 'twas pain to leave.
> *   *   *   *   *   *
> Believe me, Spencer, while I winged the hours
> Where Schuylkill winds his way through banks of flowers,
> Though few the days, the happy evenings few,
> So warm with heart, so rich with mind they flew,
> That my charmed soul forgot its wish to roam,
> And rested there, as in a dream of home.

The following lines purport to have been written on leaving Philadelphia:

> Alone by the Schuylkill a wanderer roved,
>   And bright were its flowery banks to his eye;
> But far, very far were the friends that he loved,
>   And he gazed on its flowery banks with a sigh.
> Oh Nature, though blessed and bright are thy rays,
>   O 'er the brow of creation enchantingly thrown,
> Yet faint are they all to the lustre that plays
>   In a smile from the heart that is fondly our own.
> Nor long did the soul of the stranger remain
>   Unblessed by the smile he had languished to meet;
> Though scarce did he hope it would soothe him again,
>   Till the threshold of home had been pressed by his feet.
> But the lays of his boyhood had stolen to their ear,
>   And they loved what they knew of so humble a name;
> And they told him, with flattery welcome and dear,
>   That they found in his heart something better than fame.
> Nor did woman—oh woman! whose form and whose soul
>   Are the spell and the light of each path we pursue;
> Whether sunned in the tropics or chilled at the pole,
>   If woman be there, there is happiness too;—
> Nor did she her enamoring magic deny;—
>   That magic his heart had relinquished so long,—
> Like eyes he had loved was *her* eloquent eye,
>   Like them did it soften and weep at his song.
> Oh, blessed be the tear, and in memory oft,
>   May its sparkle be shed o 'er the wanderer's dream;
> Thrice blessed be that eye, and may passion as soft,
>   As free from a pang, ever mellow its beam!
> The stranger is gone—but he will not forget,
>   When at home he shall talk of the toils he has known,
> To tell, with a sigh, what endearments he met,
>   As he strayed by the banks of the Schuylkill alone!

It was also during his lonely rambles on the banks of the Schuylkill that the following beautiful ballad stanzas were written—most probably while contemplating some neighboring cottage:

> I knew by the smoke, that so gracefully curled
>   Above the green elms, that a cottage was near;
> And I said, "If there's peace to be found in the world,
>   A heart that was humble might hope for it here!"

THE SCHUYLKILL FROM LAUREL HILL LANDING.

>   It was noon, and on flowers that languished around
>   In silence reposed the voluptuous bee;
>   Every leaf was at rest, and I heard not a sound
>   But the woodpecker tapping the hollow beech-tree.
>   And "Here, in this lone little wood," I exclaimed,
>   "With a maid who was lovely to soul and to eye,
>   Who would blush when I praised her, and weep if I blamed,
>   How blest could I live, and how calm could I die!"
>   By the shade of yon sumach, whose red berry dips
>   In the gush of the fountain, how sweet to recline,
>   And to know that I sighed upon innocent lips,
>   Which had never been sighed on by any but mine!

Whatever may be thought of the justness of Mr. Moore's estimate of our country forty-five years ago, it hardly needs comment now. The poet, then young and inexperienced, lived long enough to form different and more correct opinions. It is but a few months since he died, after lingering, for a considerable time, in a melancholy and imbecile state of mind. Whatever his sentiments may have been, subsequently to his visit to this country, as to the state of American civilization, literature, and the arts, is now perfectly immaterial;— for, as a nation and a people, we have lived long enough to *learn a little*, and have not been without opportunities of illustrating our progress. We have paid our respects to old England in various ways, and at sundry times;—and there can be no doubt but that she *knows us*. Whatever our progress *is*, she finds it no child's play to keep up with us, whether on *land* or *sea*. As for poor Ireland—she, too, has heard from us, and whether we be "savages," "democrats," or "poets," she probably has a correct idea of the extent of our *productive resources*, if not of our *benevolence*. The spirit that can prompt generous feelings in one case, can supply it in all cases. No matter what the bard thought of *us*, *we* had a good opinion of him; and the day will never dawn when American hearts will cease to beat to his happy strains.

After leaving the cottage, we pass on to the Falls of Schuylkill, some six miles from the city. On our right, on the other or eastern side of the river, is Laurel Hill Cemetery, one of the most lovely and inviting spots of the kind in this country. So popular has this necropolis of the dead become, that the company has been obliged to increase its area, and several adjacent tracts of land have accordingly been added to it. Many strangers own lots in this beautiful Cemetery, and some of its handsomest tombs and monuments have been erected over the remains of eminent men who served their country in important public capacities. We give an accurate view of a portion of the grounds from an original sketch just taken, as also a view of the grand entrance.

ENTRANCE TO LAUREL HILL.

The Falls of the Schuylkill were so called, because, in former times, before the erection of the Fairmount dam, they were quite perceptible, but have since entirely disappeared.

The Reading Railroad makes a fork at this point—one branch crossing the river by a splendid bridge, and extending to Port Richmond on the Delaware; the other branch extending to the city, over which we have just passed. The road to PORT RICHMOND is about five miles in length, and it is at this place that the great bulk of the coal brought down by the Reading Railroad is shipped. The facilities for this purpose are of the most extensive and admirable character. The wharves are extended a considerable distance into the river, over

SCENE IN LAUREL HILL.

PORT RICHMOND.

which the railroad is prolonged into numerous lateral branches, supported on strong tressel-works. The loaded cars are hauled to the water's edge, where large apartments are erected for the storage of the coal. These apartments lie under the tressel-works, the bottoms of which descend, with a slight inclination, over the water's edge. The contents of the cars are discharged from the bottom, (being constructed expressly for that purpose,) and the coal falls directly into the proper apartments below, assigned for the different sizes and qualities. A vessel, therefore, to be loaded, has merely to be drawn up to the wharf, under the projecting spout of the coal apartments, when a wicket is raised, and the coal issues out in one continuous stream. The operation of unloading the car, and of loading a vessel, is consequently very simple ; yet the contrivance, in its original conception, is one of great practical merit, saving annually, as it does, a large amount of money and time. The engraving illustrates the process just described, at the same time that it conveys an idea of the extent of the business of shipping the coal at Port Richmond. The Reading Railroad, after many years of hard struggling, has laid down a foundation for future success as broad, and practical, and comprehensive, as it was possible for human industry and ingenuity to devise. The earnings of the company, amidst all its former embarrassments, were, in a great measure, necessary to its complete equipment. To make it *productive*, accommodations corresponding with the stupendous trade of the road had to be provided; and this, too, in the midst of its darkest and most trying history. But the improvements are now made and completed, and stand forth as shining monuments to the energy and well-directed management of the road.

On our return to the Schuylkill, we shall diverge into the city, and "see what is to be seen" on the Philadelphia and Norristown Railroad, which, on the opposite shore of the river, runs parallel with the Reading Railroad from the Falls to Norristown, and embraces nearly every object of interest between those two places. The first object that strikes us, in connection with this road, is a new, elegant, and imposing one, viz.: the depot situated at the corner of Ninth and Green streets. This handsome edifice has just been completed, at a cost of some $10,000. It is, in many points of view, a model of architectural skill—combining the practical with the ornamental, at the lowest possible cost. The business of this road, extending from

PHILADELPHIA AND NORRISTOWN RAILROAD DEPOT.

Philadelphia to Norristown, with a branch to Germantown, is rapidly increasing, and has been the instrument of scattering along the route it traverses an active, intelligent, and enterprising population. The trade, of course, is mainly local, including the conveyance of passengers. Many of the business men of Philadelphia have summer residences in the vicinity of the road, while others permanently reside in the country. These, added to the ordinary movements of the dense population along the route, make the conveyance of passengers an important item, which must annually increase with the progressive increase of business. The road, a short distance from the city, passes over the Port Richmond branch of the Reading Railroad, and soon after appears at the point from which we diverged, viz: the Falls of Schuylkill, a view of which is annexed. The extensive buildings lying at the western end of the village, between the railroad and the river, comprise the chemical works of Messrs. Weightman, Harrison & Co. The greater portion of the population is supported by these large and splendid works, the proprietors of which have an establishment, equally extensive, in the city. Philadelphia is justly distinguished for its chemical productions, and the firm above mentioned probably stands at the head of this description of manufacture—one of the most complicated and arduous, we may add, that human industry and capital could embark in.

FALLS OF SCHUYLKILL CHEMICAL WORKS.

The vicinity of the Falls is much frequented, in the summer time, by the citizens of the town. They ride out here to obtain an airing. The romantic and picturesque Wissahickon empties into the Schuylkill a short distance above the village, and this is the principal source of attraction. Its banks are bold and rocky, overgrown with stately trees, whose shade affords a cool retreat from the heat, and dust, and parched and sultry avenues of the city. There are several hotels, or places of refreshment, both in the village and on the Wissahickon, and there is no lack of *material* to gratify or amuse the visitor. The drive from the city is very refreshing—the road being remarkably smooth, and studded all along with handsome cottages and tasteful scenery, as well as objects of historical and general interest. It is

THE HIGH BRIDGE ACROSS THE WISSAHICKON.

customary to enjoy the ride late in the afternoon, before dusk, while many drive out to partake of the celebrated "catfish and coffee," and return by "the light of the moon." Riding by horse-back, both for ladies and gentlemen, is in these days one of the requisites of a polite education;—and the taste for the exercise is indulged to the fullest extent—though there is still a corresponding number of vehicles, some of them splendid equipages, to be met on the road. Pic-nic parties are very frequent in this quarter, and the arrangements of the Norristown Railroad are no less complete for their accommodation than the attractions of the grounds.

The engraving on page 41 exhibits a view of the Norristown Railroad bridge across the Wissahickon, near its junction with the Schuylkill. The bridge is a fine specimen of architecture, and viewed in connection with the adjacent scenery, is probably one of the most picturesque scenes to be found in this quarter of the State. It stands seventy-five feet above the level of the water, and is about three hundred feet in length. The entire route of this rail-road, from Philadelphia to Norristown, is full of beautiful and varied scenery, nearly every inch of which is identified, in some way or other, with historical associations more or less interesting. From Fairmount to Manayunk, there is a succession of smiling villas, handsome grounds, and unique cottages,—while the hum and rattle of the loom and the shuttle, the clinking of the hammer, the grit of the saw-mill, the steam and blaze of the numerous iron works and manufactories, no less than the general life and bustle of the way-side, keep the visitor continually on the *qui vive* of excitement.

About one mile beyond the Wissahickon is MANAYUNK, situated on the east side of the river. It is the seat of very extensive and varied manufactures — embracing cotton and woollen factories, flour and paper mills, furnaces, machine shops, &c. The town owes its origin and onward progress entirely to the facilities afforded by the Rail-road, and the Schuylkill canal, which passes directly through the principal street, and supplies the water-power for all its manufacturing establishments. Some of these establishments are among the oldest in the United States, having been commenced in 1819, upon the completion of the canal, and when the present site of the place was overgrown with trees and wild bushes. At that time, Manayunk, with some other points lower down, was an excellent spot for shad-fishing;—but since the erection of the dams in the Schuylkill, this splendid fish has ceased its periodical visits to these waters, and the business, once very considerable, is now entirely discontinued.

The present population of Manayunk is probably about seven thousand—almost every person, of both sexes, being engaged in the industrial interest of the place. It was our desire to have presented a view of the interior of a cotton factory, and for that purpose, in company with our artist, we waited on one of the principal factors in that place. Without deigning to see us, he refused to give us admission, and the refusal was couched in terms so sharp and contemptu-

MANAYUNK.

ous, that it naturally suggested a few thoughts as to the moral and social tendencies of the factory system in our country. We never before realized to the extent we did on this occasion, the haughty and austere manner, the cold, biting dignity, which a commanding position over two or three hundred poor operatives, is calculated to impress on some individuals. While we are free to admit the advantages which these establishments are capable of conferring, it is not to be disguised that, in the hands of some men, they may be converted into engines of great social oppression. The spirit of enterprise which induces our citizens to make large investments in the industrial pursuits, cannot be too highly admired and extolled ; but the motives which subsequently turn some of them into uncouth and selfish nabobs, are altogether unworthy the character of a gentleman or a republican.

The most prominent evils attending the factory system in this country, are the natural results of *capital*, combined with a *speculative purpose*, to which the factory is made subservient and subordinate. Thus, an individual with a capital of one hundred thousand dollars, purchases a favorable location for a factory—no matter what kind—which is to employ from one to three hundred operatives. The location we will suppose to comprise one hundred acres of land, for which five thousand dollars are paid cash, and the remainder upon a credit of twelve months. The factory buildings are now commenced, which will absorb fifteen thousand dollars—one-half to be paid cash, the remainder upon credit. In the meantime, the tract of one hundred acres is laid off into town lots, and twenty or thirty tenements erected, at a cost of four thousand dollars—one-half cash. Thus far about $28,000 have been expended, of which one-half is credit. From ten to thirty thousand dollars are yet required to equip the factory with the necessary machinery,—say $20,000, and we have a total expenditure of upwards of $50,000. There now remains a capital of $50,000 additional to purchase stock, and as a fund to carry on the mill, which is set in *operation at high wages* for the operatives, and under favourable auspices to attract mechanics, labourers and tradesmen to the village. A brisk demand for houses and lots ensues, and the greater the demand the greater becomes the value—*ergo*, in a short time probably more than one hundred thousand dollars will have been realized from the sales and rents of houses and lots, and thus, without reference to the immediate productions of the factory, a handsome fortune has been realized from a comparatively small investment. As soon as this manœuvre is terminated, and when the village is filled to repletion, another card is to be played. The factory cannot be conducted with profit under high rates of wages—the prices of labor must be reduced, or the works suspend operation. Here ensues a panic—a general stagnation of all the affairs of the village. Many will sell out their houses and lots at a sacrifice, and move away; others will seek new employments, while, in the meantime, some will work on at *reduced wages*. The speculator now again makes his appearance, and it is not long before a large number of lots are in his possession, and thus, probably to a less extent than before, the same speculation is acted over.

We would not create the inference that our factory system generally is under the influence of such speculative movements; but we mention this as one of the evils which have hitherto surrounded it, and which have, in a great measure, crippled its operations, and raised an amount of political opposition which could not, under other circumstances, exist. But, independent of this, there are other objections, arising from the centripetal agency of such establishments in attracting around them the necessary operatives, always constituting a population more or less numerous. As this population is solely dependent upon the "lord of the loom," it is liable to be thrown into idleness at his whim or caprice, and thus a general depreciation of their condition and prospects ensues, while frequently industrious and virtuous families are exposed to want and suffering. Labor is not only degraded by such means, but it is robbed of its just reward, and, as a natural consequence, children of both sexes are driven, by the necessities of their condition, into the factory, where they earn a bare subsistence at the same time that they secure premature graves. It is impossible to contemplate the condition of these operatives without arriving at the conclusion that there is something morally wrong in the system, as well as socially inconsistent with the spirit of our institutions.

ANTHRACITE FURNACE ABOVE MANAYUNK.

A short distance above Manayunk is one of the most extensive anthracite furnaces in Pennsylvania. It is situated on the east bank of the Schuylkill, and presents a spirited scene when viewed from the Reading Railroad, on the opposite side of the river, especially in the evening, when the flames issue from the chimneys illuminating the whole establishment in their red glare. These works have been in operation for several years, notwithstanding the recent depression of the iron market, which prostrated a large number of furnaces in the valley of the Schuylkill. As we shall elsewhere make some remarks in reference to the manufacture of iron, we must forbear touching upon that point in this connection.

With the exception of the natural scenery along the Schuylkill, there is little of interest or importance until we reach the great limestone region which traverses a large area of the south-eastern counties of Pennsylvania. This limestone formation is a continuation of the great valley of Chester county, and constitutes, by far, its most important feature. It occupies a position in the stratified primary group, and teems with narrow belts and valleys, adapting it for successful culture as well as for excavation. The largest beds of limestone are met above Spring Mill, and alternate in subordinate ridges and valleys of denudation for some distance above Norristown, where the hills of the Mine Ridge, somewhat flattened down, rise through and cut off the basin. The limestone is not uniform in quality, but the lime produced from it is, upon the whole, highly esteemed, and probably the best argument in its favor is the immense quantity annually produced and shipped for the supply of Philadelphia and

LIME KILNS NEAR SPRING MILL.

other points more distant. At various points along the Schuylkill, especially near Spring Mill, Conshehocken, and Port Kennedy, there are very extensive quarries, where kilns have been erected for burning the stone—the canal and railroads, on both side of the river, affording excellent facilities for transporting the lime to market, as well as for supplying the kilns with fuel. The lime kilns are large and substantial, but erected without much regard to ornament. They are generally placed on the slope of a hill, so as to allow the limestone to be hauled to and thrown in at the top. The stones, as placed in the kiln, form an arch over the hearth, with sufficient space between the alternate layers of stone and coal to permit the heat to penetrate and decompose them. The stones are thus thoroughly roasted, and in due time crumble into powder or small white particles, in which state the lime is in a marketable condition.

SPRING MILL receives its name from a superb spring, which bubbles up with great force in the midst of a beautiful grove of trees. The water is as clear as crystal, through which the pebbles at the bottom, some thirty feet, can be distinctly seen. It is quite cold in the warmest weather.

Limestone is the general name applied to all massive varieties of carbonate of lime, that form beds of great extent, or mountains. Calcspar is carbonate of lime in its purest state. It is generally transparent or translucent, the faces of the crystals sometimes very brilliant, but the bases of the hexagonal prism are always opaque. Its color varies, sometimes perfectly colorless, often of a topaz or honey yellow, and sometimes grey or reddish. Exposed to the blowpipe, carbonate of lime does not swell nor fall to powder, but becomes white and caustic—it is then *quick-lime;* some varieties are phosphorescent when heated, and shine with a pale yellow light. *Satin-spar* consists of fine parallel fibres, either straight or waved, and has a silky lustre ; it fills small veins in limestone rock, the fibres laying across the vein. There is a particular kind of limestone containing a large proportion of bitumen, which, when rubbed or scratched by any hard substance, or slightly heated, gives out a strong fetid odor. *Chalk* is carbonate of lime of an earthy texture. It forms the cliffs along the south-east coast of England, which acquired for that island the name of Albion. Chalk formations are not often met with in the United States, though it probably exists to some extent. *Rockmilk* resembles chalk, but it is much more tender. It is found in the clefts of mountains, where it is deposited by water containing calcareous particles. *Stalactites* are sometimes transparent, and have the crystalline structure of calcspar; sometimes they consist of parallel layers of different shades of color. This rock is often employed for vases and slabs, under the names of *alabaster* and *onyx marble.* *Stalactites* are constantly forming in nearly all rich limestone formations of a cavernous structure. In the district of Port Kennedy, a few years ago, an extensive cavern was reached, where the process of the accumulation of stalactitic matter was illustrated. They are produced from the drippings of minute particles of calcareous matter, from water which percolates through the roof or sides of the rocks. When a small quantity of moisture arrives at the inner surface of the roof, before a drop is formed sufficiently large to fall by its own weight, a portion of it evaporates, and a rim-shaped film of solid matter is left adhering to the rock. Every succeeding drop increases the thickness of this film, until at length a slender tube is formed, which is constantly increased in thickness as well as in length. In general, the interior is quickly filled up, and becomes perfectly solid; but sometimes the stalactites are hollow throughout a great part of their length. At Port Kennedy, where the process of formation had been interrupted while yet in its incipient stages, the stalactites coated the interior rocks with irregular thin fibres, in some cases forming conical arches, with borders of variegated color, and in others forming pyramids on the floor. The cavern was an object of considerable curiosity during the brief period it was open to visitors, and its numerous chambers presented an aggregate area fully equal to many of our largest public buildings. A concert was held in one of its largest *saloons*, on the fourth of July, 1846, at which several hundred persons were present.

The limestone formations of this State, at numerous points, afford several varieties of superior marble. The eastern portion of the state, drained by the Schuylkill, is particularly rich in this valuable mineral, and finds a cheap and easy outlet to market. Much of the marble used for building purposes, as well as for monuments and articles of furniture, is obtained within a range of from ten to twenty-five miles around Philadelphia. The extensive buildings comprising the Girard College, were in part constructed from marble obtained in this neighborhood. There are several productive quarries in Lancaster and other counties; but those of Chester and Montgomery are the most extensive and abundant. Some of these quarries are over one hundred and fifty feet in depth, and powerful levers are used to hoist the massive pieces from their beds. At Conshehocken there is an extensive marble mill, where the rough pieces are sawed into patterns to suit the demands of the market. It is worthy of remark, that the edges of our limestone basins usually afford a marble of conglomerated character, beautifully variegated in color, similar to a variety of the Potomac marble, or to that constituting the interior pillars of the House of Representatives at Washington. This marble is a sedimentary deposit, the various pebbles being cemented together by the calcareous matter of which it is composed. Though extremely hard, it is, in some places, susceptible of the finest polish, and the reflection of the atoms upon the polished surface, at first glance, gives the impression of *roughness*, which is only dispelled by rubbing your hand upon it. A fine deposit of this peculiar rock lies near Bainbridge, in Lancaster county; also near Reading, in Berks county, while it is elsewhere met with along the borders of our limestone beds, in the vicinity of slate and shale.

This extensive region of limestone, which occupies, in numerous distinct belts or basins, a large portion of the area of what is termed the Atlantic slope is also associated with several useful metals, as the ores of copper, iron, lead, chrome, &c. The region of copper is principally north of the Mine Ridge—(the first chain of elevation met with proceeding in a north-west course,) and outcrops at various points in Pennsylvania, between New Jersey and Maryland, which States it also penetrates. The most extensive deposit is probably in Adams county, where ample preparations for mining have recently been made, in the immediate vicinity of Gettysburg. Mining explorations were also conducted, until lately, in the vicinity of Pottstown, but the ore was not found to be sufficiently productive to justify the continuation of the enterprize. More recently, operations have been commenced near Valley Forge, and the probability is, that they will prove successful. In various other points attention has been directed to this vast mineral formation, and the time is evidently not far distant, when the eastern portion of Pennsylvania will be as noted for its mines of copper and lead, as other parts of the State now are for their inexhaustible and extraordinary deposits of coal and iron.

Native Copper.—Like most of the native metals, it crystallizes in the octahedral system; but perfect crystals are seldom met with. It occurs sometimes in very large masses, but most frequently in branching and leaf-like forms, scattered among the veinstone, or penetrating it; and the surface of these ramifications is often thinly coated with green carbonate of copper, or tarnished with a brown color. In general it is very nearly pure copper, and has the color, hardness, and malleability of the refined metal, as we are accustomed to see it—sometimes it contains a minute proportion of silver.—(Varley's Mineralogy) Lake Superior is the most extensive region in the world for the production of native copper. In some parts of that region, the copper is penetrated by threads of pure silver, and grains of the same metal are scattered through it—a circumstance which has never been observed elsewhere. Its softness and ready solubility in every kind of acid, and in ammonia, distinguish copper from the few metallic minerals which at all resemble it. Copper is one of the metals that has been known and worked from the earliest period;—alloyed with tin, its hardness is much increased; and this alloy proved the various kinds of bronze of which armor, weapons, knives, and other tools were manufactured by the former inhabitants of both the old and the new continent. Axes and knives from the tombs of the ancient Peruvians and Mexicans, chisels found in the quarries of Egypt, and Roman and Gaulish swords of great antiquity, have been analyzed, and found to contain from 75 to 96 per cent. of copper alloyed with tin.—(*Ib.*) In the mines of Lake Superior tools and implements, and marks of previous workings, have been found, which can only be attributed to a race far anterior to the present era of the human family. The mines of New Jersey were worked by the first settlers long anterior to the Revolution.

Ruby Copper.—(*Red Oxyde of Copper.*)—This substance is of a fine crimson color, sometimes almost black, with vitreous lustre, ranging from semi-transparent to nearly opaque. It is brittle, and about as hard as fluorspar, with a specific gravity of 5·6. It is often intermixed with native copper, but seldom with the other ores of this metal. *Tile ore* is a variety which is intermixed with oxyde of iron and other impurities, and forms thin flattish masses, something like dark colored tiles.

Black Oxyde of Copper—which is more oxydated than the preceding species, occurs in the form of a fine black powder, or in small masses of an earthy texture, with some other copper ores. Both this and ruby copper are easily reduced on charcoal to metallic copper.

Sulphurets of Copper.—There are several combinations of sulphur with copper, some of which are valuable ores. *Copper Glance*—or vitreous copper ore—has a dark steel gray color, and when freshly broken, a perfectly metallic lustre; but the exterior is often black and dull. It is most generally found in masses without any regular form, or filling small veins. This is the richest of all the sulphurets of copper, affording 75 per cent. of metal, and being in general very free from any other. It has been met with in some of the Cornish copper mines, but only in small quantity—but in the Ural mountains it is an object of extensive exploitation, occurring there in nodules of various sizes, disseminated in veins of clay and gravel.

Variegated Copper Ore.—This was long considered to be the same substance as copper pyrites, of which the surface was tarnished; but it differs from it in containing less iron and sulphur, affording about 60 per cent. of copper, while copper pyrites does not yield more than 33 or 34. It is softer than the latter, and the color much redder—and it is less easily fusible than copper glance.

Copper Pyrites.—(*Yellow Copper Ore*)—is the most abundant of the English copper mines. Its color is that of brass, and its lustre perfectly metallic and shining, particularly when fresh broken. It is easily scratched by a knife; differing, in this character, from iron pyrites, which is much harder. Groups of small crystals are often sprinkled over other substances, as quartz, calcspar, fluorspar, galena, and blende. When pure, copper pyrites consist of sulphur 35·87, copper 34·40, and iron 30·47. Copper pyrites form veins in granite, slate, and other rocks, sometimes filling them entirely, sometimes distributed in irregular masses varying in size, and occasionally weighing some hundreds of pounds.

Gray Copper Ore.—The composition of this ore varies exceedingly in different localities; but it still presents nearly the same appearance—a light gray metallic substance. It consists principally of sulphuret of copper, antimony, and iron, with arsenic, zinc, or silver, and sometimes with all these metals—the proportion of the latter, in some instances, amounts to seventeen per cent., when the ore is worked for the sake of the silver as well as the copper.

In the same region traversed by the limestone,—(or rather in the valley above the Mine Ridge—) lead is found outcropping at different points. The ores are of various kinds, and in some cases comprise *galena*, with a plentiful mixture of silver. Extensive mining operations have lately been commenced in the vicinity of Phœnixville, Valley Forge, and Perkiomen; while the veins of the basin have been traced, here and there, over portions of the counties of Bucks, Montgomery, Chester, and Lancaster. The ore is, for the most part, pyromorphite—(phosphate of lead) a beautiful mineral, but not very abundant at any one district, though it appears to be plenty here. Its color rises from bright grass-green to yellow, orange, brown, and sometimes a dull violet. Most specimens contain nine or ten per cent. of the chlouret of lead—sometimes arseniate, and those of an orange color, chromate of lead. The chromates are found in great abundance in the Mine Ridge, in Lancaster county, of which we shall hereafter take occasion to speak. The ores are found in other spots in various stages of combination with other substances. In Bucks county, plumbago has long been mined to a considerable extent, and there is every reason to suppose that this interesting mineral, like the others, occupies a large portion of the peculiar formation in which it is found.

Native Lead is of rare occurrence. It has been observed in small grains and laminæ in some volcanic products, and, also, in some specimens of galena. It may be distinguished by its softness and sectility from the galena, which is hard and brittle. Minium (red oxyde of lead) is a red substance, occuring in the form of powder in some veins of galena and calamine. It is the same substance as the red lead used in painting; but for this and other purposes it is prepared artificially.

Yellow Oxyde of lead, which is less oxydized than the preceding ore, occurs sometimes as a powder, sometimes in solid masses, not unlike yellow jasper; its great weight distinguishes it from all other minerals which otherwise resemble it.

Arseniate of Lead takes the same forms as the phosphate of lead, but the prisms are often swelled in the middle, so as to have something of a *bowl shape;* color, generally pale yellow brown, and lustre often silky.

Carbonate of Lead—(White Lead ore.)—This is the same substance as the white lead of commerce, which is prepared artificially. It is abundant in some lead mines, filling large veins or intermixed with the other ores, either compact, earthy, or crystalline. Its crystals are derived from a light rhombic prism, differing very little from that of arthente, and are often grouped so as to form a cross or star. It is the only mineral which equals the diamond in brilliancy; its lustre, when pure and transparent, being adamantine. When fused by the blow-pipe on charcoal, a bead of lead is obtained; or if dissolved in nitric acid, upon immersing a piece of zinc (the surface being quite clean) metallic lead will quickly be precipitated on it in brilliant laminæ. When massive it has sometimes a crystalline structure, splitting readily into large flakes, with a brilliant surface. An earthy variety resembling chalk in its appearance is common in some lead mines. But it is a mineral met with not only in lead mines: it is frequently found with copper pyrites and blende. In these situations it often forms columnar masses, with a silky lustre. The sulpho-carbonate of lead, which is this substance combined with about one-third of its weight of sulphate of lead, resembles it in brilliancy and weight, but when dissolved in nitric acid, it leaves a residue, which is sulphate of lead. *Molybdate of Lead* crystallizes in square octahedrons, or very short prisms of four or six sides, of a dull yellow color, and translucent, which contain sixty-four per cent. of oxyde of lead. Sulphate of lead, in its general appearance, resembles the carbonate of lead, but is rather softer and less brilliant, and may always be distinguished from it by not effervescing with any acid. *Copreous* sulphate of lead has been found in a few places,—it is colored by the copper it contains.

Galena—(Sulphuret of Lead,) may generally be recognised by its crystallizations, and its very perfect cleavages, parallel to the faces of a cube, as well as by its pure lead-gray color. The surface is often dull, but the fracture always brilliant, and it is so brittle that cleavages may be obtained by a very slight blow. The same crystalline structure prevails where the galena is massive, sometimes resembling that of statuary marble; more rarely it is granular, or compact, with scarcely any lustre. Its specific gravity is 7·5 to 7·7. It is easily fused, giving off sulphureous fumes, and affording a globule of lead. Some galena is combined with sulphuret of silver. When this is in sufficient quantity to render it worth the expense of separating the silver, it is called *argentiferous* galena. In order to know whether galena contains any silver, dissolve a little in nitric acid, and dip into the solution a piece of copper; the silver, if there be any, will be deposited as a white metallic film on the copper.

Bournonite is a sulphuret of lead, copper and antimony—the former amounting to forty per cent.

Graphite (Plumbago, or black lead.) The substance called black lead is well known to most persons; but few, perhaps, are aware, that when they make use of a black lead pencil, they draw with a substance which is nearly identical with the *diamond*. It appears to be carbon, differing from it, when pure, only in the state of aggregation of its particles; it often contains a small portion of earthy matter, or of iron; but as the latter amounts sometimes to only one or two per cent. both are now generally considered as accidental impurities. Graphite has always a metalic lustre, with sometimes a fine scaly structure, and soils the fingers when handled. Specific gravity 2 to 2·45. It occurs in several places in the United States, and no doubt a large quantity is deposited in the slaty formation traversing Pennsylvania. For the best pencils, it is used without any other preparation than that of sawing it into thin strips, which are afterwards enclosed in wood, or formed into thin rods for ever-pointed pencils; but great numbers of pencils of inferior quality are made of a mixture composed of black lead dust, intermixed with clay, and sometimes with lamp black, or sulphuret of antimony.

Near the village of Conshehocken, the Schuylkill assumes a most beautiful appearance; the banks, on both sides, are lined with stately trees, and foliage bending to the water's edge, while the stream is as smooth and clear as one broad sheet of glass. On the

LANDSCAPE ON THE SCHUYLKILL.

one side we have the Norristown Railroad and the Schuylkill Canal, and on the other the Reading Railroad, over which are seen passing an almost endless procession of black coal-trains, and as they wind around the projecting knolls, and intervening valleys, a great rumbling noise is heard, amidst the shrill whistle of the locomotive;

the canal-boats lazily creep along, while around, as far as the eye can see, glorious nature spreads out in rich waving harvest-fields, and rolling elevations, with here and there a cluster of houses nestled amid the luxuriant scene.

The village of CONSHEHOCKEN, though of recent origin, is quite an interesting and important place. It is supported solely by several manufacturing establishments, which are carried on in its midst, and which have sprung up under the facilities afforded by the lines of improvement, no less than the rich and varied resources adjacent. Of these, there is an extensive rolling-mill for the production of sheet-iron, and its manufactures are scarcely excelled by any similar article imported, having a close resemblance to the celebrated sheet-iron of Russia. There is a very large marble-mill, which has already been alluded to, with several workshops of different kinds, and smaller extent; while a company of enterprising men has just been organized to embark in the manufacture of a new description of useful ware. They intend to manufacture, principally from the lava of the furnaces in the vicinity, a description of glass for mantels, tables, and various ornamental purposes; and as the productions can probably be afforded at low rates compared with marble, and will prove equally durable, if not equally beautiful, there is a reasonable probability that this will ultimately form a distinguishing feature of the place, if it does not originate an entirely new branch of trade.

Between Conshehocken and Norristown, there are several extensive anthracite furnaces, as well as manufactories of various kinds. The banks of the river, on both sides, present many beautiful residences, and elegant, well-cultivated farms, while the scenery generally is of that soft and genial character, relieved occasionally by a rocky declivity or gently sloping hill, that pleases the eye of the observer, while it impresses him with the spirit of activity everywhere displayed.

NORRISTOWN, the county-seat of Montgomery, seventeen miles distant from Philadelphia, is one of the most beautiful boroughs in the United States. It lies on the east bank of the Schuylkill, rising to a gradual elevation from the water's edge. The streets are well drained, the houses substantially built, (many of them unusually elegant) the citizens remarkably intelligent, the society excellent, the location healthy, the general aspect that of an industrious and enterprising population, and, in short, the whole minutiæ of the borough is such as to render it one of the most attractive with which we are ac-

NORRISTOWN.

quainted. It contains several very extensive cotton and woollen factories, iron foundries, rolling-mills, and machine shops, with numerous other industrial establishments, of more or less extent, nearly all of which are located on the river bank, and are supplied, like Manayunk, with a splendid water-power from the canal. The present population is probably between eight and ten thousand, and must greatly increase in the future under ordinary circumstances of favor. A brighter day than we have known for the last five years is, we think, about to dawn upon our workshops. We hope so, at any rate.

Norristown was formerly included in the township of Norriton, comprising a manor belonging to William Penn. The land on which the town now stands was subsequently owned by several parties, when it finally came into the hands of Wm. M. Smith, who, in 1784, laid it out into town lots. During the revolution it was occupied as a farm, and belonged to a certain John Bull, who, notwithstanding his name, was a thorough-going Whig, and the British, on their way to Philadelphia, paid him the passing compliment of burning down his barn. A short distance below the town, on the banks of the river, are still to be seen the traces of former entrenchments or breast-works, thrown up by Gen. Du Pontel, by order of Washington, at a time when he expected the British to cross the river at this place.

The first canal improvement undertaken in the United States, was commenced at Norristown, about the year 1792, of which the outline features are still to be traced. The project contemplated both a navigable water course, and a water works for Philadelphia. For this purpose, the canal was to be carried to Philadelphia on *one level*, without locks or outlets. After completing several miles of the heaviest part of the work, and spending over $400,000, the company became embarrassed, and were compelled to abandon the enterprize, many of the principal parties having themselves been involved in commercial and financial ruin. The company, however, was afterwards consolidated into the Union Canal and the Schuylkill Navigation, of both of which we shall presently have something to say.

Montgomery is one of the richest and most favorably situated counties in Pennsylvania. In all the elements of real wealth and true prosperity, it is unrivalled. The soil consists principally of limestone and red shale—the latter performing well under good tillage, with the addition of the lime close at hand. The soil is traversed by several fine streams, of which the Schuylkill, comprising the greater portion of its southwestern boundary line, is the principal; the others next in importance being the Perkiomen and its branches, the beautiful and romantic Wissahickon and its branches, the Pennepack, Tacony, Neshaminy, and others—all of which afford excellent water-power. There are at this time not less than thirty merchant, one hundred and twenty grist, seventy-six lumber, eight marble, twenty paper, thirty-five oil, twelve clover, and about the same number of powder mills, in Montgomery county; besides which, there are fifteen or more iron-works of various kinds, twenty-five large cotton factories, ten woollen factories, twelve fulling mills, and some thirty-five tanneries. This, for a county comparatively small in area, exhibits a productive capacity not easily surpassed.

The county is supplied with some of the best turnpike roads and stone bridges to be found anywhere in Pennsylvania. One of these bridges (that over the Perkiomen) cost over $60,000, and was built nearly fifty years ago. The people seem early to have realized the importance of good roads, and an immense amount of money was freely expended to make them of the best and most durable character. This principle should always be acted upon by the constituted authorities, for nothing contributes more to the lasting benefit, or enhances property to a greater extent, than good roads and bridges.

The first settlers of Montgomery county were principally Welsh, with a few Germans and English. The Germans gradually dispersed to the northern part of the county, where the language is still spoken to some extent. The Welsh, or their descendants, have long since abandoned their native language, in favor of the predominating English. The early settlers comprised some of the best men who ever landed on our shores—remarkable for their morality, industry, intelligence, and uniform respectability of deportment. The oldest place of worship now standing in Pennsylvania, was erected by them near the present town of Manayunk, in 1695. It was a Friends' meeting-house, and is still occupied by that respectable society.

We have thus, somewhat briefly, given an exposition of some of the leading features of this interesting and remarkable valley, from the Falls of the Schuylkill to Norristown. Both sides of the river, we have previously remarked, are traversed by railways, running parallel with the Schuylkill navigation. The extensive manufacturing establishments, receiving their driving-power from the river, are all located on its eastern side, which will account for its dense population and busy aspect, as compared with the opposite shore, traversed by the Reading railroad. It is this fortuitous circumstance which creates the sole trade of the Norristown railroad, at the same time that it materially aids the Reading railroad;—for while the one is in the exclusive enjoyment of the local miscellaneous trade, the other has an abundance of tonnage in supplying a large portion of the fuel consumed. We should judge that at least fifty thousand tons of coal are annually transported by the Reading railroad for the supply of the lime-kilns and ordinary consumers, between Norristown and the Falls. The two railroads, therefore, (as well as the canal) are auxiliary to each other's success.

For the reason referred to, we have little of interest to note, between the points designated, on the western side of the river. The scenery, in general, is attractive; but owing to the splendid works of man, it has more of an artificial stamp, than the usually broader and more impressive one of Nature. The tunnel above Manayunk—the Schuylkill Navigation, with its numerous locks, and dams, and bridges—the towns and villages, with their busy work-shops and towering factories—the numerous lime-kilns, furnaces, and mills—the turnpike roads, with their ponderous teams and carts; the railroads, with their snake-like trains; the electric telegraph, with its lofty poles stretching out, single file, in magnificent procession; the canal-boats, with their faithful, tugging horses, and sun-burnt crews—all evince the restless activity of man, and proclaim his glory to the passing observer.

Leaving Norristown, we cross the Schuylkill by a splendid wooden bridge (indicated in the engraving), eight hundred feet in length, and again join the Reading railroad, which henceforth traverses every town and village on our route. Here, indeed, is a sprightly little village before us, just embarking in the world. It is but yesterday since "it set up," and already we find it a considerable town, under the name, style and title of Bridgeport. The Reading Railroad is the guardian and patron of the little fellow, and under its friendly auspices it will grow and thrive, until it becomes a good-sized, old-fashioned borough.

After leaving Bridgeport, four miles beyond, we reach the village of Port Kennedy, of which we have already spoken in connection with the production of lime, constituting its sole trade. Two miles beyond this place is VALLEY FORGE. Here every inch of ground is sacred to the cause of liberty and patriotic suffering. There is not a heart in America—there is not a lover of liberal institutions anywhere, that will not swell with mingled awe and admiration, as he contemplates the scenes and incidents with which this region is identified. Here was concentrated, in the darkest hour of the revolution, the sole reliance of freedom against oppression; here were centered our hopes and our fears—here were quartered, amid the snows and blasts of a severe winter, without clothing, and almost without food, sick, famished, barefooted, and dying, Washington and his army.

REDOUBT AT VALLEY FORGE.

Valley Forge derives its name from a forge which stood near the mouth of valley creek, some time previous to the revolution. The grounds occupied by the largest portion of the encampment comprised both sides of the hill, south-east of the stream. The name of this hill is Mount Pleasant, and of that on the other side of the stream, Mount Misery. These terms were bestowed by William

VALLEY FORGE.

Penn, who, on one occasion, lost his way on the latter hill, and having regained it on the former, bestowed the names accordingly. Several extensive redoubts and breast-works were thrown up at sundry places, some of which, on the south-eastern side of the hill, are yet distinctly visible, and of which the engraving on page 58 conveys a correct idea. These works consist of large embankments of earth, arranged one after the other, along the slope of the hill, so that, in case of attack, the men could remain behind them, secure from the fire of the enemy. These breast-works, moreover, were surrounded with deep ditches, thus rendering the approach of the enemy hazardous amidst the fire of the soldiers within the redoubts. The redoubts now lie in the depths of the forest, but their outlines, as well as the former sites of the miserable huts of the soldiers, are still distinctly visible. The head-quarters of General Washington were in a

WASHINGTON'S QUARTERS AT VALLEY FORGE.

small stone house, which stands near the railroad, and from which a good view of it is afforded. A slight addition has recently been made to the back buildings, which originally consisted only of a small kitchen, erected by Washington himself. The room occupied by the General had a secret closet, in which he kept his official papers. In other respects the house is quite small, and without interest.

Washington moved with his army to this romantic spot soon after the battle of Germantown. He had previously been following the British in their movements along the Schuylkill, and finally attacked them at that place. It was after this engagement, therefore, that he took up his winter quarters in this place—a step which was dictated by the best motives of prudence and the public good.

"His soldiers," says Mr. Day, "were too ill-clothed to be exposed to the inclemency of that season under mere tents; it was therefore decided that a sufficient number of huts or cabins should be erected of logs filled in with mortar, in which the troops would find more

ENCAMPMENT AT VALLEY FORGE.

comfortable shelter. The army reached the valley about the 18th of December. They might have been tracked by the blood of their feet, in marching barefooted over the hard, frozen ground between White-marsh and Valley Forge. They immediately set about constructing their habitations, which were disposed in the order of a military camp, but had really the appearance of a regular town. Each hut was 16 feet by 14. One was assigned to twelve privates, and one to a smaller number of officers, according to their rank. Each General occupied a hut by himself. The whole encampment was surrounded on the land side by intrenchments, and several small redoubts were built at different points. A temporary bridge was thrown across the river, to facilitate communications with the surrounding country.

The army remained at this place until the ensuing summer, when the British evacuated Philadelphia.

This was the most gloomy epoch of the revolution. For many weeks the army, although sheltered from the wind, endured extreme sufferings from the want of provisions, blankets, and clothing. The Commissary's department, through neglect in Congress, had been badly managed, and on one occasion the supplies of beef were actually exhausted, and no one knew whence to-morrow's supply would come. Gen. Washington says, "For some days there has been little less than a famine in camp. A part of the army have been a week without any kind of flesh, and the rest, three or four days. Naked and starving as they are, we cannot enough admire the incomparable patience and fidelity of the soldiery, that they have not ere this been excited to mutiny and dispersion. Strong symptoms of discontent have, however, appeared in particular instances." Such was the scarcity of blankets and straw that men were often obliged to sit up all night to keep themselves warm by the fire, and many were too ill clothed to leave their huts! The want of wagons and horses, too, was severely felt for procuring supplies, and almost every species of camp transportation was performed by the men without a murmur, who yoked themselves to little carriages of their own making, or loaded their wood and provisions on their backs. The small-pox threatened those who had not been inoculated. Provisions continued to grow more and more scarce; the country had become exhausted by the constant and pressing demands of both armies, and no doubt many provisions were concealed from the Americans by the disaffected tories, who found a better market at Philadelphia, and better pay in British gold, than in continental money. Washington stated that there were in camp on the 23d December, not less than 2898 men unfit for duty by reason of their being *barefoot and otherwise naked*, besides many others detained in hospitals, and crowded into farmer's houses, for the same causes. Happily for America, there was in the character of Washington something which enabled him, notwithstanding the discordant materials of which his army was composed, to attach both his officers and soldiers so strongly to his person, that no distress could weaken their affection, nor impair the respect and veneration in which he was held by them. To this is to be attributed the preservation of a respectable military force under circumstances but too well calculated for its dissolution.

In the midst of these trying scenes, a strong combination was formed against Washington, in which several members of Congress, and a very few officers of the army were engaged. (See Reading.) Gen. Gates, exulting in his laurels recently gained at Saratoga, Gen. Lee, and Gen. Conway, (neither of them native Americans!) were at the head of this movement, and the strongest attempts were made to involve Gen. Lafayette into it also, but he openly and promptly avowed his attachment to Washington, and spurned the insidious efforts to supersede him in favor of Gates. The result of this base conspiracy is well known—it did not injure Washington, while it consigned the authors to the contempt of the public. Conway, the principal party in the affair, an Irishman by birth, was called to account, and finally died from the effects of a wound received in a duel with Gen. Cadwallader. Gates never could give a satisfactory explanation of his conduct, and the consequence is a blur on his reputation, which no previous or subsequent act of his has been able to obliterate.

It was during the encampment at Valley Forge, that the brave and kind-hearted Baron Steuben joined the American army—a position having been vacated by the subsequent resignation of Gen. Conway. Steuben, as is well known, was one of the most thorough military disciplinarians in Europe, and it was through his talents and instructions that our men acquired a facility and precision in military tactics which soon after enabled them to carry the Revolution to a glorious termination. Mr. Headley, in speaking of Steuben, says: " A more sorry introduction to our army, for one who had served in Europe, could not well be conceived. He had found our cities in possession of a powerful enemy, and when he came to look for the force that was to retake them, he saw only a few thousand famished, half-naked men, looking more like beggars than soldiers—cooped up in miserable log huts, dragging out the desolate winter amid the straw. As the doors of these hovels opened, he beheld men destitute of clothing, wrapping themselves up in blankets, and muttering complaints against Congress, which could treat them with such injustice and inhumanity. He was astonished, and declared that no European army could be kept together under such sufferings. All discipline was gone, and the troops were no better than a ragged horde, with scarcely the energy to struggle for self-preservation. There was hardly any cavalry, but slender artillery, while the guns and accoutrements—a large portion of them—were unfit for use. Our army had never before been in such a state, and a more unpropitious time for Steuben to enter on his work could not have been selected. Nothing daunted, however, and with all the sympathies of his noble nature roused in our behalf, he began, as soon as spring opened, to instruct both officers and men. His ignorance of our language crippled him at first very much; while the awkwardness of our militia, who, gathered as they were from every quarter, scarcely knew the manual exercise, irritated him beyond measure. They could not execute the simplest manœuvre correctly, and Steuben, who was a choleric man, though possessed of a soul full of generosity and the kindliest feelings of human nature, would swear and curse terribly at their mistakes, and when he had exhausted all the epithets of which he was master, would call on his aid-de-camp and ask him to curse in his stead! Still the soldiers loved him, for he was mindful of their sufferings, and often his manly form was seen stooping through the doors of their hovels, to minister to their wants and relieve their distresses.

It was his practice to rise at three o'clock in the morning, and dress his hair, smoke, and take a cup of coffee, and at sunrise be in the saddle. By that time also, if it was a pleasant day, he had the men marching to the field for their morning drill. First, he would place them in line, then pass along in front, carefully examining their guns and accoutrements, and inquiring into the conduct of the subordinate officers. The fruit of his labor soon appeared in the improved condition of his men, and Washington was very much impressed with the value of his services. Owing to his recommendation he was made Inspector General. This branch of the service now received the attention it deserved, and discipline, before irregular, or practised only under particular leaders, was introduced into every portion. All the arrangements, even to the minutest, were planned and perfected by Steuben, and the vast machinery of our army began to move in harmony and order. He had one company which he drilled to the highest point of discipline, as a model by which to instruct the others. The result of all this was seen in the very next campaign, at the battle of Monmouth. Washington there rallied his men when in full retreat, and brought them into action under the very blaze of the enemy's guns. They wheeled like veteran troops into their places, and then moved steadily on the foe.

For some time previous to his encampment at Valley Forge, Gen. Washington had his head-quarters at Whitemarsh, in Montgomery county, (a few miles east,) a view of which is here afforded. The

WASHINGTON'S HEAD-QUARTERS AT WHITEMARSH.

whole surrounding country is full of incidents connected with the movement of the army in this vicinity, and all have more or less interest to the American reader; but we agree with the poet, that—

> The camp has had its day of song—
> The sword, the bayonet, and the plume,
> Have crowded out of rhyme too long
> The plough, the anvil, and the loom.
> Oh, not upon our tented fields
> Are Freedom's heroes *bred alone;*
> The *training* of the *worskhop yields*
> More heroes true than war has known.
> Who drives the bolt, who shapes the steel,
> May, with a heart as valiant, smite,
> As he who sees a foeman reel
> In blood before his blow of might!
> The skill that conquers space and time,
> That graces life, that lightens toil,
> May spring from courage more sublime
> Than that which makes a realm its spoil.

Valley Forge contains a cotton factory, with some other minor manufacturing establishments, and has had a considerable accession to the population during the last few years. It is surrounded with a rich and populous agricultural district, in which are located several furnaces and iron works. The copper formation before alluded to outcrops here, and there is, besides, a considerable quantity of iron ore in the adjacent hills. The observatory on the summit of the hill was erected by Charles H. Rogers, Esq., the liberal-minded proprietor of the land and the cotton factory. It commands a magnificent landscape scene. The beautiful valley of the Schuylkill, richly carpeted with greensward and soft foliage, and traversed by several streams whose bridges rise above the swelling harvest-fields, stretches out before the eye. Far off the blue Kittatinny range is seen, into whose hazy atmosphere the picture gradually fades. The Schuylkill river, at the foot of the hill, winds gracefully around a broad projecting alluvial flat, beautifully shaded with tall trees, and fringed with wild bushes, very nearly in the centre of which stands the princely country house of Dr. Wetherill, and nearer the river the country mansion of John Price Wetherill, Esq. The *spirit* of the scene is greatly enhanced by the noise of the coal trains passing over the railroad, and which is echoed to the surrounding hills—no less than the view afforded of the trains themselves, often embracing one hundred and thirty loaded cars, each containing between four and five tons of coal! If any one desires to be impressed with the idea of stamina--of real greatness—of enterprise—let him stand on a commanding eminence, and behold a coal-train, nearly half a mile in length, rumbling and tearing by with extraordinary speed! But stand in the observatory and drink in the whole glorious scene—rich, and varied, and beautiful beyond description. Could unhappiness dwell amidst such plenty—such luxuriance—such inspiring incidents? It ought not; yet man is weak—

> Had he been made, at nature's birth,
> Of only flame or only earth,
> Had he been formed a perfect whole
> Of purely *that*, or grossly *this*,
> Then sense would ne'er have clouded soul,
> Nor soul restrain the sense's bliss!
> Oh, happy, had his light been strong,
> Or had he never shared a light,
> Which shines enough to show he's wrong,
> But *not* enough to lead him *right*.

Four miles above Valley Forge, and twenty-seven from Philadelphia, is the borough of PHŒNIXVILLE, situated in the valley of French creek, at its junction with the Schuylkill. Phœnixville is a very pleasant borough, containing a population of some thirty-five hundred—of whom probably eight hundred are engaged in its industrial establishments. Probably the first nail-works in this part of the country were erected here, where the creek affords a fine head of water. After having passed through the hands of three or four different parties, the works, upwards of twenty-five years ago, came into those of Messrs. Reeves & Whittaker.

The present style of the firm at this place, is Reeves, Buck & Co.—Joseph Whittaker having retired a few years ago. His son, Dr. Joseph Whittaker, retains an interest however, and is one of the managers of the works. Joseph Whittaker lives in the stately mansion directly opposite the rail-road depôt, on the opposite side of the river. We believe he has partially retired from the more active pursuits of the trade—merely "keeping as many irons in the fire" as is consistent with his old-fashioned notions of leisure. He has some works, of small extent, in view of his residence, and a furnace or two near Easton; while two of his sons have an establishment at Havre-de-Grace, Md. The Phœnix Company (Reeves, Buck & Co.) own the iron establishments at Bridgeton, and the nail-works at Cumberland, N. J., besides those at Phœnixville;—while Mr. Reeves is the senior partner of the firm of Reeves, Abbot & Co., proprietors of the splendid railroad mill and iron works at Safe Harbor, in Lancaster county. The mill at that place, in connection with the one located here, produced all the iron used in constructing the Central Railroad; and it is not the least interesting feature of that road, that its rails are the most substantial and reliable of any similar route in the United States.

PHŒNIXVILLE IRON WORKS.

The works at Phœnixville embrace several extensive anthracite furnaces, machine-shops, rolling-mills, nail and cotton factories, etc., among which is the splendid establishment for the production of railroad iron. A visit to these extensive iron-works cannot fail to prove highly interesting — especially the railroad mill, where some two hundred men are employed. We shall describe the whole process of iron manufacture in connection with the trade of the Juniata, and beg leave to refer the reader to our book on the Central Railroad route for information on this subject.

A railroad from this place to Harrisburg, *via* Ephrata and Cornwall, and traversing the valley of French creek, is now being surveyed. The road will connect with the Reading railroad, and the Norristown Railroad below. That the enterprise will prove successful, there can be little doubt; as, in addition to the local trade of the route, it will probably become the favorite thoroughfare of travel to the West, and thus strip the State railroad of one of its most important resources. However, the business of the interior is increasing with such rapidity, that there will soon be enough for both railroads. This route will be the shortest, as well as the most attractive for travellers, and for that reason, will be preferred. It never can do much business in the transportation of coal, because the route cannot afford sufficient gravitation to carry the extraordinary loads so peculiar to the Reading railroad. This feature of the Reading railroad renders it, in respect to the transportation of coal, the most wonderful improvement of the age.

There are several very good schools and academies in the vicinity of Phœnixville, and it is worthy of remark that while Chester and some of the adjoining counties are celebrated for the number and excellence of their seminaries of learning, a large portion of their support is derived from the Southern States. These counties are nearly all under the influence of the peculiar social and religious tenets of the Quakers, and though their political sentiments are sometimes contaminated with sectionalism—the ghastly monster that is now gnawing the vitals of our Nationality—yet, in their social and moral deportment, there is everything to admire. Intelligent and educated themselves, their benevolence of character, rigid discipline, and simplicity of manner, added to their known frugality, industry, and peaceful habits—give them peculiar qualities for the

> Delightful task! to rear the tender thought,
> To teach the young idea how to shoot,
> To pour the fresh instruction in the mind,
> To breathe the enlivening spirit, and to fix
> The generous purpose in the glowing breast.
> Oh speak the joy! ye, whom the sudden tear
> Surprises often, while ye look around,
> And nothing strikes your eye but sights of bliss,
> All various nature pressing on the heart;
> An elegant sufficiency, content,
> Retirement, rural quiet, friendship, books,
> Ease and alternate labor, useful life,
> Progressive virtue, and approving Heaven!

The Chester or Yellow Springs are situated but a few miles from Phœnixville, and are approached by mail stages. This watering-place formerly enjoyed a high celebrity, and is still visited to some extent; but numerous similar establishments, springing up in every part of the country, have no doubt materially diminished its ancient attractions.

But it is time to leave this busy and pleasant village—pleasant to us with many recollections of the past—dear, as the residence of one of our most esteemed friends, " whose life is gentle," and, like lord Brutus, " the elements so mixed in him, that all Nature might stand up, and say, with a universal voice, this is a *man!*" But there are others—one of them a distinguished Poet and Traveller, who, even now, is traversing the broad desert plains, amidst the scorching climes of Asia—prominently associated with our " recollections" of Phœnixville. It was here that Bayard Taylor, while editor of the village paper, laid a portion of the broad and substantial foundation which is to support his present and his future fame. The beautiful valley stream, we are sure, will always retain a snug place in his memory; sporting on its clear, calm surface, with a cluster of admiring friends, the bright evenings were made musical. Rowing " by the light of the moon,"

<blockquote>Our oars kept time, and our voices kept tune!</blockquote>

After a considerable voyage, during which the poet would entertain us with incidents of his unpublished " travel's history,"—interspersed with the jokes, criticisms, and gossips of others of the adventurous party—we would reach the "head of navigation" and land upon the green sloping banks, which are sprinkled with gay wild flowers, and shaded with tall majestic trees. Here the perfume of the well-tilled harvest fields, borne along in the cool evening breeze, saluted the grateful senses; and then, with one accord, all would plunge into the stream,

<blockquote>Whose crystal depth
A sandy bottom shows,</blockquote>

and lave its pure bright waters until, late in the evening, and fatigued with the labors of the expedition, we sought

<blockquote>Tired nature's sweet restorer—
Balmy sleep.</blockquote>

Thus flew the happy, merry summer evenings when Taylor was a village editor, and when the fair prospect of a future glorious career was budding, and gradually opening out before him. Success to thee, poet!—thou more than poet—soaring eagle!—hail!

Proceeding on our tour, we pass through a tunnel, a short distance above Phœnixville, which is over 2000 feet in length. It is cut through a solid dark-red sandstone rock, and is probably one of the

TUNNEL AND BRIDGE ABOVE PHŒNIXVILLE.

heaviest sections of railroading ever executed in the United States, as, in fact, the entire road may be regarded as one of the most extraordinary, in many respects, in the world. Emerging from the tunnel, and crossing the splendid and substantial stone-arched bridge, the scenery is entirely changed. Here the eager eye may take in a glorious landscape. The Schuylkill, winding around the projecting hill through which we have passed, describes a half-circle in a distance of little more than a mile. As far as the eye can see, a broad and luxuriant valley, lying between gently sloping hills, stretches out, through which wanders the river. The scene is rich in its development of agricultural fertility, and the green fields sparkle with the neat and comfortable habitations of the farmer.

> From the moist meadow to the withered hill,
> Led by the breeze, the vivid verdure runs,
> And swells, and deepens, to the cherished eye.
> The hawthorn whitens; and the spicy groves
> Put forth their buds, unfolding, by degrees,
> Till the whole leafy forest stands displayed,
> In full luxuriance, to the sighing gales.

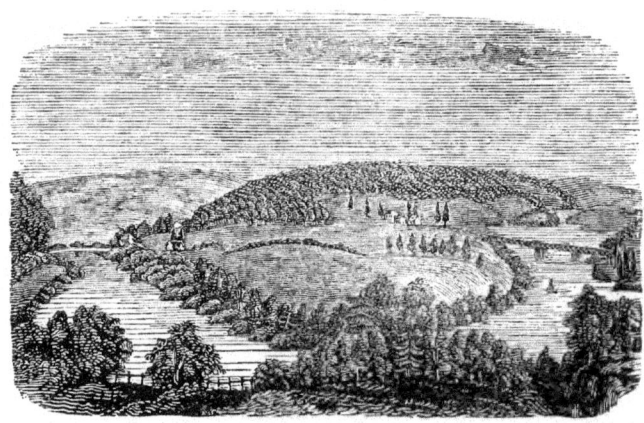

LANDSCAPE.

Passing the stations of Royer's Ford, 32m. and Limerick, 34m. we reach the borough of POTTSTOWN, forty miles from Philadelphia. It is very pleasantly situated, in a rich undulating country, on the right bank of the Schuylkill. The houses, which are generally plain but comfortable, are built principally upon one broad street, lying above the railroad, and lined with numerous gardens and shade-trees. The scenery of the country is very fine, but has nothing of the boldness mingled with it which characterizes some other spots along this river. The valley is here equally as fertile as it is below, and the Manatawny creek, crossed by a romantic looking old stone bridge, and emptying into the Schuylkill, furnishes the driving-power of several extensive flour and saw-mills. The Schuylkill navigation passes along on the opposite side of the river.

Pottstown derives its name from John Potts, who held a large tract of land in this quarter, including that upon which lies the town. West of it, beyond the Manatawny, is a stately but unique stone mansion, commanding a view of the valley, which was erected by him before the revolution. It was at that time the admiration of the people, and they came from a great distance around to look at it! Mr. Potts was an enterprising speculator in iron-works, and had an establishment in each of the adjoining counties of Chester and Berks.

POTTSTOWN.

He was a descendant of Thomas Potts, who early settled at Burlington, N. J., and was the father of Isaac Potts, who erected the iron-works at Valley Forge, from which that place derives its name. His son, Isaac, was at that time sole owner of the land where Pottsville now stands, but sold it long before it was known to contain coal. This tract afterwards came into the hands of a German named Potts, some of whose descendants still reside there, and we may probably allude to them again, in speaking of the coal formation, and the trade which it has originated. The population of Pottstown may be estimated at two thousand. There are several quite handsome churches, two large boarding schools, &c. The machine shop, and car factory, belonging to the company, are quite prominent and imposing buildings.

The extensive copper formation already spoken of, has several outcrops near this borough, where mining operations were prosecuted several years ago. The ore, however, was not rich enough to justify the continuance of the enterprize. We are not sure whether the ore proved deficient in quality, or whether the difficulties of mining it were too great and expensive to pay. Operations have, however, been discontinued for the present.

After leaving Pottstown, we soon enter the county of Berks—a rich and populous county, originally settled by Germans, and still more or less under the influence of its primitive characteristics. The general aspect and quality of the soil is rich, and its fertility is maintained, in the absence of scientific principles elsewhere called to aid, solely by *hard labor*. The first lesson (and often the only lesson) a Berks county farmer teaches his children, is upon the subject of labor, accompanied always with practical illustrations. The philosophy of the "shovel and de hoe," the plough, the harrow, and the team, is thoroughly expounded. It is no uncommon sight to see the father in the field plowing, with a little boy, scarcely able to walk, sitting on the horse, with a whip; while it is equally as common to see boys of fourteen guiding the plough, and turning over as pretty and graceful a furrow as could be desired. The old principles of cultivation are thus inculcated and handed down from father to son; and education—scholastic, social, or moral—has thus far had very little influence upon them. Like their fathers, they neither read nor travel—but believe in religion, democracy, and General Jackson.

An anecdote is recorded of two Berks county farmers, which exhibits the awkward simplicity of their business transactions. The individuals were neighbors, and frequently borrowed small sums of money from each other, which was promptly paid back at the specified time. They lived thus for many years, and both prospered by their indefatigable industry. At length one of them was compelled to provide himself with a new and larger barn, and as his "available" means did not quite suffice, he concluded to call on his old neighbor for the balance. His request was promptly complied with, and, after the money had been paid over, it was prudently suggested by the borrower himself that a promissory note should be *received*, "so as dat he might know dat de money must be baid." The note was drawn, whether *payable* to the bearer or not, we do not know—but it was mutually concluded that, as he had *received* the money, and was to return it at the specified time, he was the proper person to take charge of the note, which he did!—thus reversing the usual order of things. Time flew round, and, promptly at the time specified, the borrowed money was restored, and with it the note, so "dat de lender might know as dat the money haf been baid!"

Douglassville, 44½ m. and Birdsboro', 49 m. are two unimportant stations on the road.

Between Pottstown and Reading, there are several very pretty landscape scenes, which the observant traveller will not fail to notice. When within a mile or two of the latter place, the railroad winds along upon the side of a high precipitous hill, and penetrating a stratum of hard rock, irregular fragments of which are left standing by the side of the road, in bold and craggy peaks. Below the railroad, in almost perpendicular descent, flows the Schuylkill, which gracefully winds round a projecting mound of land on the opposite side, and reflects, in its clear and unruffled surface, the dark moss-covered rocks and wild bushes overhanging its banks. Winding swiftly around this mountain spur, we emerge into a wide valley or basin, hemmed in with high and sloping mountains, at the foot of which the city of READING is situated. The city is a beautiful and healthy place, and has long been the retreat of strangers and travellers during the summer months. During the revolution, while the city of Philadelphia was constantly intimidated with sudden incursions from the enemy, Reading was the principal place of resort and refuge. Here some of the most distinguished citizens of the commonwealth temporarily established themselves. The effect of their

RAILROAD CURVATURE NEAR READING.

presence and social intercourse with the citizens, was subsequently felt upon the society and general tone of the place, which is now, indeed, noted for its substantial, liberal, and comprehensive spirit, no less than the social good feeling, hospitality, and intelligence of its citizens, individually; for while the people of the county cannot generally be complimented for their intelligence, it must not be inferred that Reading is included with them. Nothing would be more unjust—for while it is true that the people are somewhat influenced by the tone of the country sentiment, it is equally true that the latter is also very much directed by the city; so that, considering their mutual dependency, and the *equilibrium* existing between them, it is owing principally to the popular sentiment of Reading that the people of the county have progressed, as far as they have, in education and the usages of modern society.

Reading possesses, to a very remarkable extent, all the requisites for great industrial enterprise. The agricultural resources of the county—of which it is the judicial seat—are truly enormous. The soil is drained by numerous streams of large volume, which, following the narrow alluvial valleys intervening between the mountain ranges, afford water-power of unlimited extent, and applicable to every description of manufacture. Iron ore, of various qualities, abounds throughout the whole county, and there are several rich deposits in the vicinity of Reading. The calcareous conglomerate, previously alluded to as appearing in the red shale deposits along the Mine Ridge and Blue Mountain ranges, in this county lies near the Schuylkill, in the vicinity of Reading. It is known as the "Potomac marble," and when not too hard to polish, must be considered as very valuable. Copper ore also occurs at several points, but generally in such small quantity, and so mixed with iron, as to render the expediency of working it rather doubtful. But what is most important to this city, and which has given it, within the last few years, an impulse of great industrial vigor, is the coal trade, from whose beds it is distant thirty-six miles. Added to this, is its accessibility, by canal, to the Susquehanna, and by both railroad and canal to Philadelphia and Pottsville, giving it a commanding interior position, which must ultimately be used to its great and permanent benefit.

The Union Canal, which unites with the Schuylkill Navigation at Reading, was the first canal route ever surveyed in this country, and a brief notice of some of the persons and circumstances associated with it, will probably not be without interest. George W. Smith, Esq., in an article first published in Hazard's Register, says that William Penn, in his proposals for a second settlement in the province of Pennsylvania, promulgated in 1690, alludes to the practicability of effecting a communication by water between the Susquehanna and the Schuylkill. Canals and turnpikes were unknown at this period, even in Great Britain. Numerous interesting letters of distinguished citizens are extant, which prove that the Union is indebted to this State for the first introduction of canals and turnpikes to public attention. Their views were regarded at that early period, (1750 to 1760) with but little interest in England, and excited the attention of but few in the colonies. At the present day it is difficult to determine to whom we are chiefly indebted for introducing the subject to public attention. If our information be correct, we may attribute to David Rittenhouse (the astronomer), and Dr. Wm. Smith, provost of the University of Pennsylvania, the credit of being the first laborers in this hitherto untrodden field. Afterwards Robert Morris, the financier of the Revolution, and still later Robert Fulton, the engineer, and inventor of steamboats, of whom Pennsylvania is justly proud, lent their powerful assistance. The writings of Turner,

Comac, Wm. J. Duane, and Samuel Breck, Esqrs., and subsequently of Gerard Rallston, Richard Peters, Jr., Matthew Carey, Samuel Mifflin, Wm. Lehman, John Sergeant, and others, are too well known to require enumeration. In 1762, David Rittenhouse, (and Dr. Smith, above mentioned, associated with him,) surveyed and levelled a route for a canal to connect the Susquehanna with the Schuylkill, by means of the Swatara and Tulpehocken creeks—the former emptying into the Susquehanna at Middletown, twelve miles below Harrisburg, and the latter emptying into the Schuylkill near Reading. The Union canal, which has since accomplished this object, passes over a portion of the route thus surveyed—and this is the first region ever surveyed in the colonies for a canal. The views of the projectors of this work were, if the difficulties of that period be duly considered, far more gigantic and surprising than have been entertained by their successors in any part of the Union. They contemplated nothing less than a junction of the eastern and western waters of Lake Erie and of the Ohio with the Delaware, on a route extending 582 miles! The Alleghany mountain was deemed to offer an insuperable obstacle to a continuous navigation—and to overcome this a portage was accordingly recommended;—an expedient which we, at a very recent period, were compelled to adopt, but which now, in the full era of steam locomotion, will soon be proudly overcome by our iron horses.

Duly to appreciate the enterprise of that age, we ought to consider that the great valley of the Ohio and Mississippi was almost one boundless forest, uninhabited but by the beasts of the forest, and the Indians. Attainable monied capital was then almost unknown in the colonies; the very term "engineering" was equally unknown in the vocabulary of those days. No canal was then in existence in England. Public opinion, even then, had yet to learn that canals were not visionary undertakings. The sneers of many were to be encountered; nevertheless, under all these trying discouragements, the earliest advocates for inland navigation commenced their efforts in Pennsylvania. In 1769 they induced the American Philosophical Society to order a survey for a canal to connect the Chesapeake bay with the Delaware—a work long since in successful operation. The provincial legislature, about the same period, authorized a survey of a route, extending five hundred and eighty-two miles, to Pittsburg and Erie. This survey was performed, and a report made strongly recommending the execution of the project. The adoption of the plan was only postponed in consequence of the Revolution. After the termination of that struggle, several works were commenced in North Carolina, Virginia, and Maryland. The canal through the Dismal Swamp, connecting the Chesapeake bay and Albemarle Sound, with the works on the Potomac, James, and Rappahannock rivers, were commenced and partially finished between the years 1786 and 1791. The great project of Pennsylvania was allowed to slumber until the 29th of September, 1791, about a century after William Penn's first prophetic intimation, when the Legislature incorporated a company to connect the Susquehanna and Schuylkill by a canal and slack-water navigation. Robert Morris, David Rittenhouse, Wm.

Smith and others, were named as commissioners. The intention of connecting the eastern and northwestern parts of the State is distinctly expressed in this, and a subsequent act of the 10th of April, 1792. By the terms of this last act a company was incorporated to effect a junction of the Delaware with the Schuylkill river, by a canal extending from Norristown to Philadelphia—a distance of seventeen miles, which has already been alluded to. The Schuylkill river, from the former city to Reading, was to be *temporarily* improved, and thus form, with the works of the Susquehanna and Schuylkill Company, an uninterrupted water communication with the interior of the State; with the intention of extending the chain to Lake Erie and the Ohio river. Experience soon convinced the two companies that a greater length of canal was requisite, in consequence of the difficulties of improving the channels of the rivers; hence the company last mentioned determined (in compliance with the suggestions of Mr. Weston, a British engineer, whom they had imported,) to extend *their* canal from river to river, a distance of seventy miles. In conjunction with the former company, they nearly completed fifteen miles of the most difficult parts of the two works, comprising much rock excavation, heavy embankments, deep cuttings, and several locks, which were constructed with bricks. In consequence of commercial difficulties, (in which, it is known, some of the chief stockholders were shortly after involved—including the patriot, Morris, who was, in fact, on one occasion, imprisoned for debt!) both companies were compelled to suspend their operations, after having expended upwards of $450,000. The suspension of these works, and, some time after, that of the Chesapeake and Delaware Canal, had a very disastrous effect on every similar enterprise which was projected for many years after.

Frequent abortive attempts were made, from the year 1795, to resume operations; and notwithstanding the subscription of $300,000 stock, subsequently tendered by the State, these companies continued in a languishing condition. In 1811 the two bodies were united, and re-organized as the Union Canal Company, which has ever since been the style of the company. They were specially authorized to extend their canal from Philadelphia to Lake Erie, with the privilege of making such further extension, in any other part of the State, as they might deem expedient. In 1819 and 1821 the State granted further aid by a guarantee of interest, and a monopoly of the lottery privilege. The additional subscriptions obtained in consequence of this legislative enactment, enabled the managers to resume operations in 1821. The line was re-located, the dimensions of the canal changed, and the whole work finished in about six years from this period; after thirty-seven years had elapsed from the date of the first work, and sixty-five from the date of the first survey. It is ninety miles in length, including the branch extending to the coal region at Pine Grove, in Schuylkill county. That portion between Pine Grove and Middletown, was enlarged in 1851, and is now equal to the capacity of boats running on the State canals; but the other section can pass boats of twenty-five tons only. The summit of this canal, about six miles in length, passes over a limestone deposit, and in consequence of the fissures abounding in this rock, a large portion of the water was lost. A number of experiments were tried to overcome this loss, such as lining it with clay, planking, &c. The difficulty was, we believe, entirely remedied on the occasion of its enlargement, last year, and the work may hereafter be regarded as complete in all its arrangements and in all the details of its construction, while the coal trade alone will probably soon make it a paying concern.

The Schuylkill Navigation, already alluded to in connection with the Union Canal, was incorporated as a separate and distinct concern in 1814, without mining and trading privileges, and hence it has ever been the interest of the company to invite tonnage from all sources, and in every quarter. It was originally designed for the products of the forest, the field, and the mine—all of which abounded in the counties drained by the river and its numerous tributary streams. The forests, especially, were at that period remarkable for the quality of their timber, and the height and symmetrical proportions of the trees; and, among intelligent and sagacious men, little doubt was entertained of the future importance of the coal trade, then without any existence whatever.

The Schuylkill Navigation is one hundred and eight miles in length, extending from Philadelphia to Port Carbon, in Schuylkill county. It was erected at a cost of nearly three millions of dollars. It was sufficiently complete, in 1818, to allow the descent of several boats, and tolls to the amount of two hundred and thirty dollars comprised the receipts for the season. From this year to 1825, no account was kept of the different articles for which tolls were received, and we are unable, therefore, to determine the amount of tonnage on coal descending the valley during this period. The Navigation, however, owing to the imperfection of the structure, was not in a favorable condition for the prosecution of business during any portion of this period. This arose from the obvious inexperience of the people of that day in canal-building: and obstructions of every description were of course to be expected. Of these, the most frequent were breaks in the banks of the canal, which would not only retard the progress of boats, and render the business extremely hazardous and uncertain, but subjected the Company to heavy expenses for repairs. The revenue to the stockholders was of course very limited; and at no season, we believe, previous to 1830, was it sufficient to yield a dividend of over one-half per cent.—while quite as often a *loss* would be experienced at the close of the business season.

A few years afterwards, however, (1830,) when the coal trade began to assume some importance, the stock of the Navigation yielded very handsome dividends, and continued annually to do so, until it encountered a formidable rival in the railroad, which was extended to Pottsville in 1842. From this period, the coal trade became immensely important, and the canal company determined, in 1846, to deepen the channel, and otherwise enlarge and improve their works. The canal was sufficiently enlarged to float boats of 180 tons burthen, while the number of locks was reduced from 109 to 71—eleven of which are guard locks without lift, of which the gates generally stand open, and are, in fact, closed only during freshets. The average time of passing a lock with a boat is about four minutes, at which rate all the locks on the canal could be passed in about five hours; or, making a reasonable allowance, six hours would give ample time to overcome the total descent of 620 feet—and if, at every lock, a descending boat should meet an ascending one, the whole time lost in effecting the cross passage does not exceed twelve hours. This is an immense improvement over the old navigation.

Above the Blue Mountain nearly all the canals are almost equal in width to the slack-water pools formed by the dams. Below the Blue Mountain, the water line of the canal, which is never less than sixty feet, widens frequently to one hundred feet and more. Taking these things in connection with the fact, that about half the length of the navigation consists of wide slackwater pools, and it will be observed that in point of width everything practically desirable has been attained.

Several attempts have been made to introduce steam in the navigation of the Schuylkill,—and though apparently attended with some success, have not led to any practical end, as yet. The only steamboats now plying on its waters, are those between Fairmount and Manayunk. If coal could be used for fuel—(of which, by the way, there can be no doubt,) and the machinery made sufficiently light to correspond with the tonnage of the boat, there would, indeed, seem to be no practical reason why steam should not supersede horses. The splashing of the water against the banks of the canal, occasioned by the evolutions of the paddle-wheel, presents the most potent objection;—yet this is but a trifle, and might readily be overcome, if sufficient attention were bestowed upon the subject. We look forward to the day, when Prof. Page's brilliant experiments in electro-magnetism will find practical application in the ordinary pursuits of life. His electric engine already possesses eight-horse power; and, inasmuch as the *entire machinery* consists of but a single wheel, or iron circle, this would be the exact thing to introduce for the propulsion of *canal boats*. The whole weight of an electric engine of sufficient capacity to propel *five canal boats*, together with the *fuel*, for twenty days, would not, probably, exceed three hundred pounds!

The entire length of the Navigation, as previously remarked, is 108 miles—its lockage 620 feet—the burden of its boats 180 tons—the size of its locks, 110 by 18 feet—the width of its canals, never less than 60 feet—and the least depth of water upon the mitre sills 5½, and in the clear levels 6 feet.

The five leading railroads, and their laterals, to the Schuylkill Navigation and the Reading Railroad, are the Mine Hill and Schuylkill Haven, terminating at Schuylkill Haven; the Mount Carbon, terminating at Mount Carbon; the Mill Creek, terminating at Port Carbon, and the Schuylkill Valley, terminating at Mount Carbon.

At Schuylkill Haven a very fine dock, nine hundred feet long, sixty feet wide,

THE READING RAILROAD.   81

and six feet deep, with its rail seventeen feet high above water, shute and landings on both sides, has been constructed by Mr. Dundas. This dock alone is capable of shipping, in an active season's work, at least two hundred and fifty thousand tons of coal, and is leased by the Navigation Company.

At Port Carbon, the Navigation Company have constructed an extensive series of landings. A part of these landings below the Mill Creek Railroad bridge, consists of a dock, about nine hundred feet long, sixty feet wide, and six feet deep, with its rail elevated eighteen feet above water, with shutes and landings on both sides. There is room at this landing for thirty boats of one hundred and eighty tons burden to load at once, and it is capable of shipping five hundred thousand tons of coal per annum.

In the pool of dam No. 1, the company have erected six new landings, with their rails elevated sixteen feet above the water, and so arranged that six large boats may load at once, without interruption. In addition to these, and also in the upper dam, the Navigation Company have leased and fitted up the long dock, which accommodates six large boats at the same time. Thus, the Company have a variety of fine landings to ship coal coming from the Schuylkill Valley and Mill Creek Railroads, and capable together of shipping near seven hundred thousand tons in a season's work.

In addition to the foregoing, the Company have constructed a dock and landings at Mount Carbon, similar to the Firth Dock at Port Carbon, and of about the same capacity. We shall probably again refer to these landings when speaking of the coal trade.

To guard against the danger of a deficiency of water, to which the Navigation is exposed in dry seasons, they have erected several large dams upon tributary streams at the head of navigation, from which to draw supplies in cases of deficiency. The dam at Silver creek covers nearly sixty acres, and contains about forty million cubic feet of water, which is estimated to be capable, of itself, of floating about one hundred and twenty thousand tons of coal annually!

The Reading Railroad, of which we now propose to give a brief description, was chartered on the 4th of April, 1833, and surveys were made the same year, and forty-one miles placed under contract and construction a year afterwards. The charter authorized subscriptions to the amount of twenty thousand shares, of fifty dollars each, being a capital of one million dollars, with the right to double it, if found necessary. It provided for an annual meeting on the second Monday in January, and the right of stockholders to cast one vote for every share, not exceeding two; one vote for every two shares not exceeding ten; and one vote for every five, for any amount above ten, that may belong to them in their own right or as trustees. Proxies to be dated within six months, and only to be used for purposes

L

expressly stated. No blank proxy to be good, and no third person to be substituted. The government of the road is vested in a **President** and six Managers, who are authorized to make By-laws and all needful regulations, subject to the approval of the stockholders at their annual meeting. The President and Managers have full power to manage and operate the road. Special meetings may be called, but no business can be done without a majority in interest of the stock is represented. No dividend to be declared except from the *net profits*, so that the capital shall remain unimpaired. The charter is perpetual.

It was originally designed for its present purpose, an outlet or avenue to market for the Schuylkill Coal Region; but its first charter extended only to the city of Reading, fifty-nine miles from its terminus on the Delaware River, near Philadelphia, as the right of constructing a railroad between Reading and Port Clinton, twenty miles, had already been granted another corporation, the Little Schuylkill Railroad Company, extending from Tamaqua to Port Clinton, twenty miles. From insufficient means, this company was unable to extend their road, and yielded their right and charter to the Reading Railroad Company, who, with a further extension of their charter, beyond Port Clinton to Pottsville, went into an active prosecution of the whole work, from Pottsville to the Delaware, ninety-four miles, under one charter, now known as the Reading Railroad.

Every Pennsylvanian is familiar with the great embarrassments to the business of the country, checking commercial enterprise, disastrous to every branch of industry, and fatal to public and private credit, during the period from 1833 to 1842. Notwithstanding all these difficulties, the friends of this road pushed steadily on with its construction, taxing their energies, their means and their credit to the utmost, to insure its speedy completion; and on the first day of 1842, the first locomotive and train passed over the whole line between Pottsville and Philadelphia.

The event was celebrated with military display, and an immense procession of (seventy-five) passenger cars, twelve hundred and twenty-five feet in length, containing two thousand one hundred and fifty persons, three bands of music, banners, &c., all drawn by a single engine! In the rear was a train of fifty-two burden cars, loaded with one hundred and eighty tons of coal, part of which was mined the same morning four hundred and twelve feet below the water level.

The whole was under the charge of Mr. Robinson, chief engineer, and Mr. G. A. Nichols, superintendent. The entire capital invested up to this time, including all its vast real estate, locomotives, workshops, wharves, etc., amount to *over sixteen millions of dollars.*

From that date to the present, its business, its revenue and its credit have increased, in a degree scarcely paralleled by any similar improvement, until its tonnage and its receipts are measured, as at present, by millions.

Two continuous tracks of railway extend the whole distance of ninety-four miles, from Pottsville to the Delaware river, at Port Richmond—situated three miles above the heart of the city, and one hundred and four miles from the sea, while a branch road extends from the Falls of the Schuylkill *via* Fairmount, to Broad street, in the city. This portion of the road formerly belonged to the State—but upon the completion of the road to avoid the inclined plane, the canal commissioners sold this section to the Reading Railroad company, who, with characteristic enterprise, put it into immediate repair, and laid down upon it a strong and substantial rail. They also materially strengthened and otherwise improved the railroad bridge across the Schuylkill, so that, instead of awaiting the slow process of being hauled over with horses, the passenger trains are drawn over by locomotives without delay or hindrance. This branch of the road is used altogether for the coal and miscellaneous trade of the city, including passengers.

The rail used on this road is of the H pattern, with both top edges alike, and weighs forty-five and one-eighth, fifty-two and one-half and sixty pounds to the yard; the lightest having been first, and the heaviest last used. A few tons of other rails, purchased before a further supply of the pattern adopted for the road could be obtained in England, and varying from fifty-one to fifty-seven pounds per yard, are also in use.

The track is laid in the most simple manner, the lower web or base of the rail being notched into white oak cross sills, seven by eight inches in thickness, and these laid on broken stone, fourteen inches deep, and well rammed. This method is found admirably calculated for the enormous tonnage of the road, being rapidly and economically repaired and replaced, securing a thorough drainage, and preserving its line and level true, at all seasons of the year.

The grades of this road are the chief elements of its success in revolutionizing public opinion, on the subject of the carriage of heavy burdens by railway. From the most important branch Coal-feeder of the road, at Schuylkill Haven, to the Falls of Schuylkill, a distance of eighty-four miles, the grades all descend in the direction of the loaded trains, or are level, with no more abrupt descent than nineteen feet per mile. At the Falls, an assistant locomotive engine of great power pushes the train, without the latter stopping, or any delay, up a grade of forty-two and one-half feet per mile, for one mile and a quarter, thus placing it on a *descending grade*, within four miles of Richmond, whither it is readily conveyed by the same engine which started from Pottsville, never leaving the train.

The bridges on this line are of great variety in plan, and material of construction; stone, iron and wood being used. The most perfect and beautiful structure on the road, if not in the State, is a stone bridge across the Schuylkill near Phœnixville, built of cut stone throughout, with four circular arches, of seventy-two feet span, and sixteen and one-half feet rise each, at a cost with ice-breakers, of $47,000. (See engraving—page 69.) There are seventy-five other stone bridges and culverts, varying from six to fifty feet span; all of circular arcs, spanning water courses, branches of the Schuylkill and roads. There are seven bridges from twenty-five to thirty-eight feet span each, built of iron, trussed after the Howe plan, with wrought iron top and bottom cords, wrought iron vertical ties, and cast iron diagonal braces. These bridges are stiff and light, and present a very neat and handsome appearance. As, however, the flooring is of wood, and therefore liable to decay and accident, they have only been used where the width and depth rendered stone bridges impracticable; the latter being always used in replacing wooden structures, wherever it is practicable. There are twenty long wooden bridges, varying from forty-one to one hundred and sixty feet span, built on various principles, chiefly of lattice work, assisted by heavy arch pieces. Of this latter description, the bridge over the Schuylkill at the Falls is a fine specimen. It is six hundred and thirty-six feet long, consisting of four spans of one hundred and thirty-four, two of one hundred and fifty-two, and one of one hundred and sixty feet over the river. There is one bridge built on Burr's plan, with double arch pieces of one hundred and forty-nine feet span; and one on Howe's plan, one hundred and fifty-six feet span, also assisted by arch pieces. Besides the above, there are about twenty wooden bridges of short spans, from fourteen to thirty feet, built of King post, Queen post, Bowe's truss, and joists. There are also several small iron and wooden bridges.

There are four tunnels on the road. The longest of these is near Phœnixville, one thousand nine hundred and thirty-four feet cut through solid rock, worked from five shafts and two end breasts; deepest shaft one hundred and forty feet; size of tunnels, nineteen feet wide, by seventeen and one-quarter high; total cost, $153,000. Another tunnel at Port Clinton, is one thousand six hundred feet long, worked from the two ends only; material, loose and solid rock mixed; one thousand three hundred feet are arched; depth below the surface of the ground, one hundred and nineteen feet; total cost $138,000. The Manayunk tunnel is nine hundred and sixty feet long, through very hard solid rock, worked from two ends; depth below surface, ninety-five feet; total cost $10,000. Another tunnel under the grade of the Norristown Railroad, and through an embankment of the latter, is one hundred and seventy-two feet long, formed of a brick arch, with cut stone façades.

The depôts on this road are all substantially built, but with a view to use, rather than ornament. At Schuylkill Haven, four miles from Pottsville, is erected a spacious engine house, round, with a semi-circular dome roof, one hundred and twenty feet diameter, and ninety-six feet high; with a forty feet turning platform in the centre, and tracks radiating therefrom, capable of housing sixteen second class engines and tenders. The principal depôts for making up the coal trains are at Mount Carbon, Palo Alto, (situate on the Schuylkill, about one mile, in an angle, from Pottsville and Mount Carbon;) Schuylkill Haven, and Port Clinton. At all of these places, there is extensive side-railway to arrange the cars in trains, as they arrive from the numerous branch roads. Sometimes upward of one hundred and fifty *loaded cars* are attached to a single locomotive, which, at five tons to each car, gives an aggregate tonnage of seven hundred and fifty tons! No other road in the world can do this!

At Reading are located the most extensive and efficient workshops and railroad buildings of every description to be found in the country. The company's property covers, altogether, besides the railway tracks, some thirty-six acres, the greater part of which is in use for the various occupations required to keep this vast thoroughfare in life and active motion. These shops embrace various departments, in which every description of mechanical work required for the machinery of the road, can be supplied. A description of the dimensions of the several buildings is probably unnecessary—the reader will be good enough to take our assurance that they are large, very large, enormously large, and, in point of interest and extent, are second to no iron establishment in the United States. About four hundred hands (including men and boys) are employed in the establishment, which embraces an iron foundry and machine shop, brass foundry and machine shop, carpenter's shops, furnaces, smiths, and various other subordinate shops. In short, the establishment builds and repairs all the running-machinery of the road, as locomotives, cars, tenders, smoke pipes, etc., for which purpose all its waste *scrap iron* is consumed, being remelted and puddled, and thereby a great saving is effected, probably equivalent to some *fifty thousand dollars* per annum, besides the accommodation and perfect *adaptation* of the machinery to the road, which it affords. We do not know the items of cost of this establishment; but it must be regarded as one of the company's most valuable features, and it is now in complete and successful organization. To arrange the vast *details* of this road required many years of patient and persevering toil; and no words can express too strong a compliment upon the business talents of those persons under whose auspices it has finally attained its present admirable working condition.

For many years the company have been extremely anxious to introduce anthracite coal, instead of wood, as fuel for their locomotives. In point of economy, over *one hundred thousand* dollars would annually be saved, could coal be successfully substituted. Various and numerous experiments have been made, and latterly with success. Several engines, calculated to use coal, are now being constructed at their own workshops at Reading, under the direction of Mr. Mulholland. They will be completed and put on the road in a few weeks hence. They are of great capacity, and built with a view, also, to swiftness. Wood is getting scarce along the line of the road, and the introduction of coal, which can be had on the beds at a mere trifle, will prove highly advantageous to the interests of the company. The difficulty hitherto in the way of using anthracite, we may add, was the intense concentrated heat it would create, materially injuring the works of the fire-box, as well as the boiler. There never was much difficulty in burning the coal—but, under its destructive effects, there was no advantage in using it, and *all coals* are very nearly similar in this respect. They emit a heat which eats into the iron of the boiler, and, in time, renders it unfit for use. Thus a boiler, heated with anthracite, will last, say six months; one heated with bituminous coal will last nine months, and heated with wood, twelve, fifteen, or eighteen months. Now, all the money saved in the cheaper cost of coal over wood, is lost by the injury entailed on the locomotive, for the cost of a new boiler may be stated to be some two or three hundred dollars, besides the loss of time required to repair. But the difficulty can, will, and must be overcome. We know it can, and we will aver that it *will*, for the Reading Railroad Company have undertaken to do it, and with them there never has "been such word as fail."

A merchandize depot, recently completed at Reading, is one hundred and twenty-four by eighty-four feet, to accommodate that rapidly increasing branch of business. About a mile below the Reading depot, where the railroad is nearest the river, most efficient waterworks are constructed, consisting of a reservoir on the Neversink hill side, fifty-one feet above the rails, holding seven hundred thousand gallons of water, supplied by a force pump worked by a small steam-engine. Attached to this station are also two separate tracks, with coal chutes beneath, three hundred and four hundred and fifty feet long each, for the use of the town; two wood and water stations; a small portable steam-engine for sawing wood, a refreshment house for crews of engines stopping to wood or water; a brass foundry, passenger car-house, passenger rooms, offices, &c., &c. All the machinery of the main shops and foundry is driven by a very handsomely finished stationary engine, with double cranks, of thirty-five horse power, built entirely on the works.

At Pottstown station, eighteen miles below Reading, extensive and efficient shops have also been erected, chiefly for work connected with the bridges and track of the road, and new work of various descriptions. The principal shops here are one hundred and fifty-one by eighty-one, one hundred and eighty-one by forty-one, and eighty-one by forty-four feet. The first shop is covered with a neat and light roof, built of an arched Howe truss, forming a segment of a circle, seventy-eight and a half feet span by sixteen feet rise.

At Richmond, the lower terminus of the road, at tide water on the river Delaware, are constructed the most extensive and commodious wharves, in all probability, in the world, for the reception and shipping, not only of the present, but of the future vast coal tonnage of the railway; forty-nine acres are occupied with the company's wharves and works, extending along twenty-two hundred and seventy-two feet of river front, and accessible to vessels of six or seven hundred tons. The shipping arrangements consist of some twenty wharves or piers, extending from three hundred and forty-two to eleven hundred and thirty-two feet into the river, all built in the most substantial manner, and furnished with chutes at convenient distances, by which the coal flows into the vessel lying alongside, DIRECTLY FROM THE OPENED BOTTOM OF THE COAL CAR FROM WHICH IT LEFT THE MINE. See engraving, page 36. As some coal is piled or stacked in winter, or at times when its shipment is not required, the elevation of the tracks by trestlings, above the solid surface or flooring of the piers, affords sufficient room for stowing upwards of two hundred and fifty thousand tons of coal. Capacious docks extend inshore, between each pair of wharves, thus making the whole river front available for shipping purposes; over one hundred vessels can be loading at the *same moment*, and few places present busier or more interesting scenes, than the wharves of the Reading Railroad at Richmond. A brig of one hundred and fifty-five tons has been loaded with that number of tons of coal in less *than three hours time*, at these wharves. The whole length of the lateral railways extending over the wharves at Richmond will probably exceed ten miles, and affording a shipping capacity for upwards of *three millions of tons!* and it will probably not be many years before this amount, extraordinary as it may seem, (as, indeed, it really is,) will be annually transported over this great thoroughfare. The company has laid the *foundation* for a trade as broad as the future destiny of the coal trade itself.

A very convenient and neat engine-house is erected at this station; it is of a semi-circular shape, with a forty feet turning platform outside; from which tracks radiate into the house, giving a capacity for twenty engines, and their tenders, of the largest class. The building is three hundred and two feet long on the centre line, by fifty-nine feet wide. It is built in the simple Gothic style, the front supported by cast iron clustered pillows, from the tops of which spring pointed arches, and the whole capped with turretted capping. Immediately adjoining are built spacious machine and work shops, for repairs of engines and cars, all under one roof, two hundred and twenty-one by sixty-three feet. A visit to this chief outlet of the Pennsylvania coal trade will give the best idea of its magnitude, and of the various branches of industry connected with it.

The extraordinary business of this road requires, of course, a large amount of running machinery. The latter consists of about one hundred locomotive engines and tenders, including six or seven in constant use on the lateral railroads in the coal region; about five thousand iron and twelve hundred wooden coal cars, six hundred cars for merchandise, and some thirty elegant passenger cars.

The engines vary from ten to twenty-four tons weight; two very powerful engines, of twenty-seven tons weight each, are used exclusively on the Falls grade, before mentioned. The iron cars weigh over twenty-four tons when empty, and carry five tons of coal. The *average* load of each engine, during the busy months of the year, is very nearly five hundred tons of coal, (of twenty-two hundred and forty pounds.)

The total length of lateral railroads, connecting with the Reading Railroad, under other charters and corporations, but all contributing to its business, using its cars, and returning them loaded with coal and merchandize, is over one hundred miles. Some of these railroads are constructed in the most substantial manner, with the best superstructure at present used in the country.

Of these, it connects with the Mount Carbon Railroad, and the Mount Carbon and Port Carbon Railroad, at Mount Carbon one mile below Pottsville, and with the Mine Hill Railroad and its numerous radiating branches, at Schuylkill Haven, (this road is about being extended to connect with the Shamokin Railroad, thus affording a connection with the Susquehanna, and passing through the great Mohanoy coal region:—it will thus bring an incalculable amount of additional tonnage and passengers to the Reading Railroad) also at Port Clinton, with the Little Schuylkill Railroad extending to Tamaqua, and thence into several lateral branches to numerous coal districts adjacent. The roads have each many miles of branches, penetrating all the coal districts of this unparalleled region, and the greater portion of their tonnage is, and always will be, transferred to the Reading Railroad; for so firmly has it established itself into the *local arrangements of the lateral railway trade* of Schuylkill county, that it can always *command* a large portion of the trade.

Such, "my jolly companion," is a brief exposition of some of the leading features of the Reading Railroad. Look at it—starting out, with one hundred miles of railway branches, from the most extensive deposit of anthracite coal in the world, lying some seven hundred feet above tide-water—look at the road, as it winds its way amidst the rich fields and sloping banks of the Schuylkill, and gradually sinks into the bosom of the most beautiful and populous city on the American continent! One hundred miles in length, sloping gracefully from the coal-beds to the river Delaware—is not that a beautiful idea to contemplate? Nature has had a hand in it, and enterprising man has improved what she carefully prepared. She made the route, and raised the coal-beds to their present height with the express purpose, no doubt, of rendering them available to our wants. For this, all thanks!

> I'm not romantic, but, upon my word,
>   There are some moments when one can't help feeling
> As if his heart's chords were so strongly stirred
>   By things around him, that 'tis vain concealing
> A little music in his soul still lingers,
> Whene'er the keys are touched by Nature's fingers.

The ground upon which Reading is situated originally belonged to Thomas and Richard Penn, who disposed of the lots, subject to an annual ground-rent. This rent through neglect, had been left unpaid after the Revolution, and when attempted to be collected, some years ago, the accumulated amount occasioned a great deal of surprise and excitement in the place. The rent was stoutly resisted, but a compromise was soon after effected between the town authorities and the claimants. The public buildings of Reading are amongst the handsomest in the State. The Court House, the Prison, and several of the Churches, are models of architectural skill, and reflect great praise upon the liberality and taste of the citizens. Reading, says Mr. Trego, was formerly celebrated for the manufacture of wool hats, and the business is still carried on extensively; but of latter years other branches of manufactures have so much increased as to have given this ancient trade but a secondary rank. Previous to 1836, hats, boots, shoes, and stone-ware were the principal manufactures; since that time establishments have been put in operation for rolling iron, making nails, casting in iron and brass, manufacturing locomotive and stationary steam-engines, rifle-barrels, augers, &c.; a steam saw and chopping-mill, and several shops for the manufacture of thrashing-machines, corn-shellers, ploughs, harrows, and other agricultural implements. Besides these manufactories, some of which are very extensive, and employ a large number of mechanics, a cotton factory is now in operation, embracing some three hundred looms, and employing about the same number of operatives. The mill was finished a year or two ago, and is built in the most substantial as well as ornamental style—with a stock capital of some two hundred thousand dollars.

Besides producing excellent ale and porter, Reading enjoys some celebrity in connection with the manufacture of wines. The vineyards are said to be quite extensive, and the wine is certainly "not hard to take." For certain kinds of wine, we can see no reason why the banks of the Schuylkill should not prove available—the grape attaining here all the pulpy sweetness that characterizes it in some of the most favored lands. The weather, however, is too wet ever to permit the grape to attain the *dryness* so necessary for the production of the higher grade of wines;—but, under ordinary circumstances of favor, wine can be produced at least equal, if not far superior, to the horrid adulterated stuff palmed off as wine, and which, heavily charged with *impure liquor*, makes it justly obnoxious to the friends of the "Maine Law."

The common language of Berks county, and some of those lying adjacent, is an impure German, so corrupted and mixed with the more popular English words, that it would scarcely be understood by a well educated German from the fatherland. In many parts of the county, where the inhabitants seldom leave their own neighborhood, English is neither spoken nor understood; but this language is rapidly gaining ground among those of the people who have business communications with others than their immediate neighbors. It will probably not be long before English and German will be equally used, except in some secluded portions of the county.

Among the natural curiosities in the county, may be mentioned Dragon's cave, in Richmond township, which is thus described in Trego's Geography by a gentleman resident in the vicinity. "The entrance to this cave is on the brow of a hill, on the edge of a cultivated field. Passing into it, the adventurer descends about fifty yards by a rough and narrow passage, and then turns to the left at an acute angle with the passage hitherto pursued. After proceeding about thirty yards farther, he enters the great chamber, about fifty feet long, twenty wide, and fifteen to twenty feet high, in a rock of limestone. Near the end of this chamber, opposite to the entrance, is the 'altar,' a large mass of stalagmite, which rings under the hammer, and is translucent. Formations of stalactite are found in other parts of the cave, though none so large as the mass just mentioned." Sinking Spring, near the Harrisburg turnpike, five miles from Reading, is a considerable curiosity to those who are not familiar with the circumstances frequently attending large springs in a limestone region. The water here rises and *sinks again in the same basin*, which is very deep; thence finding its way again, under ground, through fissures and hidden caverns in the limestone rock, probably once more to seek the light of day in some other place. A similar phenomenon is found in Sinking Spring valley, in Blair county, which is elsewhere noticed in this work.

We have already stated that, during the revolution, Reading was (as it is now during the summer,) a place of resort for the citizens of Philadelphia. It was here that the conspiracy (for so it should be termed) against Washington was supposed to have had its birth, while the popular sentiment was by no means enthusiastic in favor of the commander-in-chief, owing, probably, to the exposed position of the frontier settlements to the ravages of the Indians, and who, in their bold incursions, rendered Reading itself sometimes obnoxious to their attacks. Alexander Graydon, who was, at that time, on parole, (having been captured by the British, near New York,) gives the following in his memoirs: "The ensuing winter, at Reading, was gay and agreeable, notwithstanding that the enemy was in possession of the metropolis. The society was sufficiently large and select, and a sense of common suffering, in being driven from their homes, had the effect of more closely uniting its members. Disasters of this kind, if duly weighed, are not grievously to be deplored. The variety and bustle they bring along with them, give a spring to the mind, and when illumined by hope, as was now the case, they are, when present, not painful, and when past, they are among the incidents most pleasing in retrospecting. Besides the families established in this place, it was seldom without a number of visitors—gentlemen of the army, and others;—hence the dissipation of cards, sleighing parties, balls, &c., was freely indulged. Gen. Mifflin at this era was at home—a chief out of war, complaining, though not ill; considerably malcontent, and, apparently, not in high favor at head-quarters. According to him, the ear of the commander-in-chief was exclusively possessed by Greene, who was represented to be neither the most wise, the most brave, nor most patriotic of counsellors. In short, the campaign in this quarter was stigmatized as a series of blunders, and the incapacity of those who had conducted it unsparingly reprobated. The better fortune of the Northern army was ascribed to the superior talents of its leader, and it began to be whispered that Gates was the man who should, of right, have the station so incompetently sustained by Washington.

"There was, to all appearance, a cabal forming for his deposition, in which it is not improbable that Gates, Mifflin, and Conway were already engaged; and in which the congenial spirit of Lee, on his exchange, immediately took a share. The well-known apostrophe of Conway to America, importing that 'heaven had passed a decree in her favor, or her ruin must long before have ensued, from the imbecility of her military councils,' was, at this time, familiar at Reading; and I heard him myself, when he was afterwards on a visit to that place, express himself to the effect, 'that no man was more of a gentleman than Gen. Washington, or appeared to more advantage at his table, or in the usual intercourse of life, but as to his talents for the command of an army, (with a French shrug,) they were miserable indeed!' Observations of this kind, continually repeated, could not fail to make an impression within the sphere of their circulation; and it may be said that the popularity of the commander-in-chief was a good deal impaired at Reading. As to myself, however, I can confidently aver that I never was proselyted, or gave in to the opinion, for a moment, that any man in America was worthy to supplant the exalted character that presided in her army. I might have been disposed, perhaps, to believe that such talents as were possessed by Lee, could they be brought to act subordinately, might often be useful to him; but I ever thought it would be a fatal error to put any other in his place. Nor was I the only one who forbore to become a partizan of Gates. Several others thought they saw symptoms of selfishness in the business, nor could the great eclat of the Northern campaign convince them that its hero was superior to Washington. The duel which afterwards took place between Gen. Conway and Gen. Cadwallader, though immediately proceeding from an unfavorable opinion expressed by the latter of the conduct of the former at Germantown, had, perhaps, a deeper origin, and some reference to this intrigue; not that Gen. Cadwallader was induced from the intrigue to speak unfavorably of Conway's behaviour at Germantown. That of itself was a sufficient ground of censure. Conway, it seems, during the action was found in a farm-house, by Gen. Reed and Gen. Cadwallader. Upon their inquiring the cause, he replied, in great agitation, that his horse was wounded in the neck. Being urged to get another horse, and at any rate to join his brigade, which was engaged, he declined it, repeating that his horse was wounded in the neck. Upon Conway's applying to Congress, some time after, to be made a Major-General, and earnestly urging his suit, Cadwallader made known this conduct of his at Germantown, and it was for so doing that Conway gave the challenge, the issue of which was his being dangerously wounded in the face from the pistol of Gen. Cadwallader. He recovered, however, and some time after went to France. While laboring under the effects of this wound, (which was at first supposed to be mortal,) he wrote a letter to Gen. Washington, apologizing for his previous conduct towards him, and expressing the highest admiration of his military career;—as I had the means of knowing that Gen. Cadwallader, suspecting Mifflin had instigated Conway to fight him, was extremely earnest to obtain data from a gentleman who lived in Reading, whereon to ground a serious explanation with Mifflin. So much for the manœuvering which my location at one of its principal seats brought me acquainted with, and which its authors were soon after desirous of burying in oblivion."

Conrad Weiser, a celebrated Indian agent and interpreter, spent the latter part of his life in Reading, where he kept a trading house. He was born in Germany, but came to this country in early life, and settled about the year 1714. He lived much among the Six Nations of New York. He was a great favorite among them, was naturalized by them, and became perfectly familiar with their language. Desiring to visit Pennsylvania, the Indians brought him down the Susquehanna to Harris' ferry, (now Harrisburg, the capitol of the State,) and thence he came across to the Tulpehocken, and thence to Philadelphia, where he met Wm. Penn for the first time. He became a confidential interpreter and special messenger for the province among the Indians, and was present at many of the most important treaties between the proprietary government and the Indians. In 1737 he was commissioned by the Governor of Virginia to visit the Grand Council at Onondaga. He started very unexpectedly, in the month of February, to perform this journey, of five hundred miles, through a wilderness, where there was neither road nor path, and at a season when no game could be met with for food. His only companions were a Dutchman and three Indians. In 1744 he was despatched in like manner to Shamokin (now called Sunbury) "on account of the unhappy death of John Armstrong, the Indian trader." On both these journeys he has specially noted interesting observations relating to a sincere and general belief among the Indians, in the interposition of an overruling Providence, and their habit of acknowledging with gratitude all such interpositions in their favor. Mr. Weiser had an Indian agency and trading house at Reading. In 1755, during alarms on the frontier, he was appointed colonel of a regiment of volunteers from Berks county. The Indians always entertained a high respect for his character, and for years after his death were in the habit of making visits of affectionate remembrance to his grave. Col. W. was the grandfather, on the maternal side, of the late Hon. Henry A. Muhlenburg, formerly Minister to Austria, and during his life one of the most distinguished citizens of Reading, where his family still reside.

The country from Reading to Hamburg is more hilly than that which we have already passed, but still maintains a high degree of cultivation. The rolling aspect of the soil, clothed in the richest verdure, affords here and there a splendid landscape; but the scenery is,

HAMBURG.

for the most part, monotonous, until we arrive at Hamburg, where we take leave, for a time, of the pleasant harvest-fields and scenes of agricultural industry, and penetrate the region of mountains. Here the Kittating or Blue Mountain range crosses our course, and, as far as the eye can see, traverses the country in bold and majestic ridges, sometimes sloping gradually into the valley below, and again rising in towering grandeur to the overhanging clouds.

HAMBURG, 75m. is situated on the left bank of the Schuylkill, near the Blue Mountain, and about a mile from the railroad. It embraces a population of about one thousand, and, being situated in Berks county, is composed mostly of Germans. The surrounding country is a rich agricultural district, and the village is at least very pleasantly situated. The trade of the place is unimportant. But let us hasten on, for—

> Our heart's in the mountain—our heart is not here,
> Our heart's in the mountain a-chasing the deer ;
> A-hunting the deer and pursuing the roe—
> Oh, our heart's in the mountains wherever we go!

The Kittating is a formidable barrier to our progress, but the railroad has a way to overcome it—or to pass through it. Plainly, the road *pierces* (no allusion to you, General, or any other democrat!) the mountain, and the first thing we see, on emerging from it, is PORT CLINTON, seventy-eight miles from Philadelphia, and about six hundred feet above the Delaware river.

TUNNEL.

Here we have a tolerable specimen of the scenery the traveller may expect for some time to come—for he is now in the midst of those bold parallel layers of mountain, broken and distorted into irregular fragments, which constitute the outlines of the great Apalachian system, and which, under various local names, traverses several States, and divides the lakes and rivers, east and west of it, into separate systems. The scenery here is bold, wild and picturesque, while the whole country looks like a vast

"Ocean into tempest tossed."

At some places, the mountain sides are steep, rising from eight to twelve hundred feet almost perpendicularly, at the foot of which flows the Schuylkill, or some of its tributary streams. The red shale, which support the outlayers of conglomerate rock, decomposes under exposure to the atmosphere, and the effects of rain, snow and frost, and the debris, borne off by the streams winding round the mountains, leave the conglomerates, and more durable rocks, reposing in awful cliffs and precipices, frequently overlooking the valleys below. Sometimes the mountains slope gradually from their base to the summit, and the harder rocks are strewn over its surface in the wildest confusion, in pieces of all sizes and shapes. The smallest of these stones are carried down the mountain sides by heavy rains, and the noise which the descending mass makes, as the stones are pushed along by the impetuous torrent, is both exciting and novel. It is thus that the narrow valleys have been gradually formed, which will be more minutely illustrated in our geological treatise, which we shall very soon commence. What can be more interesting to the eye of the traveller—to the man of care and business, "doom'd, for a certain time," to the daily rounds of city-life—than the change of scene which these bold, rolling mountains afford? Where is the invalid, accustomed to the dull monotonous scenes of level plains, or breathing the low and impure atmosphere of the populous city, who would not be invigorated, mentally and physically, in the midst of this primeval terrestrial ocean?

> Thrice happy he! who, on the sunless side
> Of a romantic mountain, forest-crowned,
> Beneath the whole collected shade reclines;
> Or in the gelid caverns, woodbine wrought,
> And fresh bedewed with ever-spouting streams,
> Sits cooly calm; while all the world without,
> Unsatisfied, and sick, tosses in noon.
>   Welcome, ye shades! ye bowery thickets hail!
> Ye lofty pines! ye venerable oaks!
> Ye ashes wild, resounding o'er the steep!
> Delicious is your shelter to the soul,

PORT CLINTON.

> As to the hunted hart the sallying spring,
> Or stream full-flowing, that his swelling sides
> Laves, as he flows along the herbaged brink.
> Cool, through the nerves, your pleasing comfort glides;
> The heart beats glad; the fresh expanded eye
> And ear resume their watch; the sinews knit;
> *And life shoots swift* through all the lengthened limbs.

Before leaving this place, which is a point of divergence, it is proper that we should have an understanding with the reader. If the traveller desires to proceed to Wilkesbarre, or to Mauch Chunk, it would be advisable for him to leave the car, and place himself in the train for Tamaqua, twenty miles distant, where stages run directly to the place mentioned. For our part, we must proceed to Pottsville, fifteen miles distant, from which place, dear sir, we'll join you at Tamaqua, and then

> Follow thee
> With truth and loyalty.

We would cordially invite you and your carpet-bag to accompany us, but that there is no railway communication between the two places, and we have a horror for stages in warm weather. So, farewell!

> If we do meet again, why we shall smile;
> If not, why then this parting was well made.
> * * *   Come, ho! away! *All a-b-o-a-r-d!*

Well, leaving Port Clinton, we go puffing, and blowing, and thundering amid the wildest mountain scenery, but still keeping by the side of the Schuylkill, which gradually becomes smaller as we approach its head waters—(though we can't see that there is anything "un'nat'ral" in the circumstance.) We pass two unimportant post stations—Auburn and Orwigsburg—the former a promising candidate for village importance, and the latter a mere off-shoot of its unfortunate god-father, two miles distant—formerly the seat of justice of Schuylkill county. Eighty-nine miles from Philadelphia is SCHUYLKILL HAVEN, containing a population of nearly three thousand. It is the principal depot for the shipment of coal, both by canal and railway. Lying in a beautiful valley, it affords the only belt of tillable land to be found in the county. The valley is long but narrow, and is dotted with numerous pleasant farms, and surrounded with bold and romantic scenery, of which the annexed figure is an illustration.

LANDSCAPE.

The Mine Hill and Schuylkill Haven Railroad commences here, and following the valley for a short distance, throws out several radiating branches, connecting the main road with all the coal operations in the Mine Hill, and Swatara ranges, embracing the rich coal districts of Minersville, Tremont, Llewellyn, Branchdale, etc. The tonnage of the road is enormous, and like the Reading railroad to which it is tributary, it has a descending grade throughout its combined length. A train of passenger cars runs between Schuylkill Haven and Tremont, *via* Minersville. The route is a pleasant and attractive one—penetrating the richest coal districts of Schuylkill county. The company have recently obtained the right to extend their road (which is among the most profitable to the stockholders of any other in the United States, at the same time that it is one of the most substantial in its structure,) over the mountain, so as to connect with the Shamokin railroad at Sunbury—thus uniting the Schuylkill with the Susquehanna at that place. It is proposed, we believe, to ascend the mountain by inclined planes, constructed in the usual manner, or upon the plan of those at Mauch Chunk, hereafter described. This route will afford an outlet for the great and prolific Mahonoy coal region, and the road will probably prove as profitable, at no distant day, as the main line, with its numerous projecting branches, now is.

Three miles above Schuylkill Haven we reach MOUNT CARBON, which was formerly the terminus of the Reading Railroad. A large quantity of coal is also shipped from this place, from which several lateral railroads extend to the coal mines in the vicinity of Pottsville, Port Carbon, St. Clair, Tuscarora, and other mining districts. The handsome cottage on the slope of the hill on the opposite side of the river, is the residence of Mr. Walker, superintendent of this section

MANSION HOUSE NEAR POTTSVILLE.

of the railroad. The stone octagonal building in front of it, is his office. On the left, and near the railroad, is the Mansion Hotel, now conducted by Mr. Head, one of the most distinguished caterers on the American continent. His reputation, in connection with hotels, is so well established, and so preëminently superior to what is ordinarily associated with country inns, that no remark of ours could add one jot to its value. While proprietor of the Mansion House in Third street, Philadelphia, his guests—always few in number—comprised some of the most distinguished and opulent citizens which the country could boast. His wines were recognized as indisputably superior to those of any public or private gentleman in the city, while his *table d'hote* literally groaned beneath the sumptuous dishes spread out upon it.

This hotel has recently been materially enlarged and improved.

It is the only establishment, in this part of the country, specially adapted for the accommodation of summer visitors to the coal region —being large and airy, and sufficiently near Pottsville to render it readily accessible, and sufficiently distant to avoid its dust and business excitements. It has an extensive and beautiful park attached, with bowling house, and other arrangements for out-door amusements. The location, as may be supposed from a glance at it, is extremely cool and pleasant in the summer, as well as quiet and retired. The nights are particularly refreshing, and sleep is to be enjoyed, after the heat of the day, with a vigor perfectly unknown in the crowded city. Some time since, the family of Iterbide, formerly Emperor of Mexico, and the family of Mr. Tucker, the distinguished President of this road—(and the Emperor of American Railway Managers) made this hotel their annual summer quarters.

POTTSVILLE, nearly a mile above this hotel, is the great theatre of the anthracite coal trade. It is situated principally on the northern slope of Sharp Mountain, which constitutes the boundary of the coal formation. The present population is about eight thousand, included in which are some of the most active merchants, coal operators, and business men to be found anywhere in the State. The citizens are remarkably intelligent and enterprising, and there is probably no place in the commonwealth where the people combine a greater amount of practical intelligence with the accomplishments of travel and scholastic learning. The evidences of their industrial energy are scattered broadcast throughout the coal region—above as well as *below* ground. Schuylkill county presents a perfect net-work of railroads and canals, and there are probably upwards of *one hundred and fifty miles* of the former laid down below the surface of the earth. At nearly every turn in the road, the stranger will hear the loud puff of the colliery steam-engines, and the shrill whistle of the locomotive resounding through the narrow valleys and passes of mountains. Pottsville itself contains several large machine-shops, as well as a railroad and bar-iron rolling mill, recently erected. All the stationary steam-engines used in the coal regions are made here or in some of the adjacent villages. The heavy machinery used in the railroad mills at Phœnixville and other places, was produced here, and it is probably a sufficient compliment to her mechanics to say, that their productions are properly appreciated where they are subject to the severest test, which is in their own immediate locality.

POTTSVILLE.

Pottsville, like all the other towns in the coal region, is of recent origin. Previous to 1824 there was scarcely a dwelling on the spot where the town now stands. The excitement which followed the discovery of coal, brought to the place a swarm of adventurous spirits, which rendered it the focus of unprecedented speculations in coal lands and town lots. In the midst of this excitement, the town took a run-and-jump into existence. It never went through the slow and gradual movements of a baby-existence; but with one tremendous bound, found itself nestling at the foot of a high mountain, swarming with hungry speculators and eager adventurers of every description—young, old, and ugly—green, black, and brown—all huddled together, and "eager for the 'fray."

The late Joseph C. Neal, who was one of the motley mass, some years afterwards, wrote the following humorous description of the speculating scenes:

In the memorable year to which we allude, rumors of fortunes made at a blow, and competency secured by a turn of the fingers, come whispering down the Schuylkill and penetrating the city. The ball gathered strength by rolling, young and old were smitten with the desire to march upon the new Peru, rout the aborigines, and sate themselves with wealth. They had merely to go, and play the game boldly, to secure their utmost desire. Rumor declared that Pipkins was worth millions, made in a few months, although he had not a sixpence to begin with, or to keep grim want from dancing in his pocket. Fortune kept her court in the mountains of Schuylkill county, and all who paid their respects to her in person, found her as kind as their wildest hopes could imagine.

The Ridge-road was well travelled. Reading stared to see the lengthened columns of emigration, and her astonished inhabitants looked with wonder upon the groaning stage-coaches, the hundreds of horsemen, and the thousands of footmen, who streamed through that ancient and respectable borough, and as for *Ultima Thule*, Orwigsburg, it *has not recovered from its fright to this day!*

Eight miles further brought the army to the land of milk and honey, and then the sport began—the town was far from large enough to accommodate the new accessions; but they did not come for comfort—they did not come to stay. They were to be among the mountains, like Sinbad in the valley of diamonds, just long enough to transform themselves from the likeness of Peter the Moneyless into that of a *Millionaire;* and then they intended to wing their flight to the perfumed saloons of metropolitan wealth and fashion. What though they slept in layers on the sanded floors of Troutman's and Shoemaker's bar rooms, and learned to regard it as a favor that they were allowed the accommodation of a roof by paying roundly for it, a few months would pass, and then Aladdin, with the Genius of the Lamp, could not raise a palace or a banquet with more speed than they!

One branch of the adventurers betook themselves to land speculations, and another to the slower process of mining. With the first, mountains, rocks, and valleys changed hands with astonishing rapidity. That which was worth only hundreds in the morning, sold for thousands in the evening, and would command tens of thousands by sunrise, in paper money of that description known among the facetious as slow notes. Days and nights were consumed in surveys and chaffering. There was not a man who did not speak like a Crœsus, even your ragged rascal could talk of his hundreds of thousands.

The tracts of land, in passing through so many hands, became subdivided, and that brought on another act in the drama of speculation: the manufacture of towns, and the selling of town lots. Every speculator had his town laid out, and many of them had scores of towns. They were, to be sure, located in the pathless forests; but the future Broadways and Pall Malls were marked upon the trees; and it was anticipated that the time was not far distant when the deers, bears and wild-cats would be obliged to give place. and take the gutter side of the belles and beauxs of the new cities. How beautifully the towns yet unborn looked upon paper! the embryo squares, flaunting in pink and yellow, like a tulip show at Amsterdam; and the broad streets intersecting each other at right angles, in imitation of the common parent, Philadelphia. The skill of the artist was exerted to render them attractive; and the more German text, and the more pink and yellow, the more valuable became the town! The value of a lot, bedaubed with vermillion, was incalculable, and even a sky parlor location, one edge of which rested upon the side of a perpendicular mountain, the lot running back into the air a hundred feet or so from the level of the earth, by the aid of the paint box, was no despicable bargain: and the corners of Chesnut and Chatham streets, in the town of Caledonia, situated in the centre of an almost impervious laurel swamp, brought a high price in market, for it was illustrated by a patch of yellow ochre!

The bar-rooms were hung round with these brilliant fancy sketches; every man had a roll of incheate towns in the side-pocket of his fustian jacket. The most populous country in the world is not so thickly studded with settlements as the coal region was to be; but they remain, unluckily, in *statu quo anti bellum.*

At some points a few buildings were erected to give an appearance of realizing promises. There was one town with a fine name, which had a great barn of a frame hotel. The building was let for nothing; but after a trial of a few weeks, customers were so scarce at the Red Cow, that the tenant swore roundly he must have it on better terms, or he would give up the lease.

The other branch of our adventurers lent their attention to mining; and they could show you, by the aid of a pencil and piece of paper, the manner in which they must make fortunes, one and all, in a given space of time—expenses, so much; transportation, so much; will sell for so much; leaving a clear profit of 000,00! There was no mistake about the matter. To it they went, boring the mountains, swamping their money and themselves. The hills swarmed with them; they clustered like bees about a hive; but not a hope was realized. Calculations, like towns, are one thing on paper, and quite another when brought to the test.

At last the members of the expedition began to look haggard and careworn. The justices did a fine business; and Natty M., Blue Breeches, Pewter-Legs, and other worthies of the catchpole profession, toiled at their vocation with ceaseless activity. When the game could not be run down at view, it was taken by ambuscade. Several bold navigators discovered that the county had accommodations at Orwigsburg, (at that time the seat of justice, now located at Pottsville,) for gentlemen in trouble. Capiases, securities, and bail-pieces became as familiar as your garter. The play was over, and the farce of " *The Devil to Pay*" was the after-piece. There was but one step from the sublime to the ridiculous, and Pottsville saw it taken!

Gay gallants, who had but a few months before rolled up the turnpike, swelling with hope, and flushed with expectation, now betook themselves, in the gray of the morn, and then the haze of the evening, with bundle on back—the wardrobe of the Honorable Dick Dowles tied up in a little blue and white pocket handkerchief—to the tow-path, making, in court phrase, "mortal escapes;" and, in the end, a general rush was effected—the army was disbanded—*sauvi qui peut?*"

The coal region, twenty-five years ago, stood in a position equally as tempting to the people of the surrounding States, and especially those of our own, as California recently did, and still does. It was a new and unexplored region, and, in the midst of the scenes which characterized it, every one thought to play a part, and receive the smiles of fortune. Many, of course, were disappointed:—but the more practical were enabled to sustain themselves, and with the aid of the improvements made in the moments of excitement and speculation, finally established themselves permanently in the successful pursuit of their business.

Pottsville is much frequented in the summer by strangers and travellers, but principally by those who, having investments in the improvements connected with the coal trade, or in the land itself, combine business with the pleasures of travel. The place, at this season, is therefore generally pretty well filled, and adds somewhat to its interest—though there is never a lack of gaiety and spirit in the society of the town. Indeed, from what we know of it, we should pronounce it inferior, in no essential, to that of any other community in the Union—characterized, as it is, by a high tone, governed by sound intelligence and fine social feelings.

The rides in the vicinity are magnificent—for while the roads are always in the midst of the wildest and most picturesque mountain scenery, they are also enlivened with the varied scenes of industry and activity peculiar to the region—little mining villages, colliery works, saw-mills, extensive forests, rocky promontories—now looking down from the tops of mountains, then from the narrow deeply-shaded valleys looking up; these, in continual and varied succession, are among the scenes to be enjoyed in a drive, in any direction, in the vicinity of Pottsville. The roads are generally very good; indeed, in many places they are unsurpassed. Nor are they, as might be supposed, very hilly; but winding around the mountains, they attain the summit without any steep ascents, and the trees and wild bushes always afford a shade, which, while it protects the road from the sun, and prevents the accumulation of dust, only renders it more inviting for the traveller.

There are, as we have already intimated, a variety of objects in the vicinity, which the stranger might visit with satisfaction. Amongst others of similar character, is Swatara Falls, situate about nine miles from Pottsville, over a beautiful summer-road. The falls, lying about a mile from the carriage-way, are accessible over a very stony path through the bushes; but the exercise required to approach them will be amply compensated by the view afforded. The outlines are sketched in the engraving from the recollection of the writer, who visited them some four years since, and it is very probable the picture is deficient in some of the minor points. It represents the stream with a full flow of water, which, however, is not peculiar to it during the dry weather of the summer. A wilder scene than is here presented we have never found, nor a cooler spot during the heat of the summer, and after the fatigue of reaching it from the road. It is often selected, with good taste we think, as the scene of Pic Nic parties, with which we have associated it in the engraving.

Inasmuch as the general character of the country will be frequently referred to in our article on the coal formation, it would be a useless repetition to extend our remarks at this place. We will, therefore, continue the journey, and meet our old friend (who has thought well enough of our good intentions to entertain him thus far,) at Tamaqua. We take the cars near Pottsville to Tuscarora, via the Schuylkill valley railroad, and thence by stage to Tamaqua. The country, as we pass along, is grand—wild—sublime, and so forth, and all that; at Tamaqua the gorge in the mountain, through which the wild little Schuylkill, like a lost child, runs on to meet her anxious maternal

SWATARA FALLS.

parent at Port Clinton—is truly magnificent. Sharp mountain rises to a lofty height in the rear of the town, and its summit affords a splendid view of the whole interior coal basin, which is here remarkably rich in its development. There are several characteristic mountain scenes along the railroad, between here and Port Clinton—did *you* observe them? Ah, it is well; it saves us the trouble of a description.

TAMAQUA is beautifully situated, and is a thriving and important place. The little Schuylkill coal and railroad company own nearly all the adjacent coal lands, embracing upwards of five thousand acres, and it is through their auspices that the town has grown into its present prosperous condition. It is of comparatively recent origin, like all the towns and villages of the coal region; but its progress in population and business has been much more rapid, at the same time that it has been substantial and durable. During the depression of business which has characterized most of the mining districts, for the last few years, Tamaqua maintained a degree of comparative prosperity; and such is its peculiar position amongst the most important elements of industrial progress, that the place, at no distant day, must become one of great commercial interest. Tamaqua lies on the railroad route connecting Philadelphia with Lake Erie; and from the importance of the road, and the natural advantages favoring its construction, no doubt can be entertained of its ultimate prosecution. A large portion of the route, in fact, is already finished—a still larger portion graded, and but a comparatively short distance yet to be graded and equipped, to complete the whole, which would thus furnish a shorter route, from Philadelphia to Lake Erie, than is afforded from New York to Dunkirk, via the Erie railroad. Six miles from Tamaqua is Summit Hill, a small mining village, the spot where anthracite coal was originally discovered, and the site of the great open quarry of the Lehigh coal and Navigation Company. This quarry has been abandoned in favor of the usual process of mining by drifts. The coal strata, on arriving at this point, converge towards each other, and appear to have been overtilted, thus forming an almost solid area of coal of great thickness. Lying near the surface, it was for many years mined in open quarry. A railroad extends from this place to Mauch Chunk, over which the coal mined in the vicinity is carried. The road is nine miles in length, and has a gradual descent from the summit of the mountain to Mauch Chunk, where the coal is transferred to canal-boats. The entire descent is, we believe, over six hundred feet. The cars thus descend by their own weight, under the charge of a conductor; and the passage down affords one of the most unique and exciting trips which the imagination could picture. The scenery—oh! the wild, the bold, the terrible mountain scenery as you pass along—swifter than the winged messengers of the air! You look around and below with a feeling half fear and half inward unearthly satisfaction! Heavens! *could* anything be more pleasing—more delightful; and then, winding round a curvature, where the cars *might* run off the track, and precipitate their enthusiastic and excited contents several hundred feet into the little agricultural valley below—you tremble and shrug, and wonder *if* anything could be more *dangerous!* A-ha! Look at those lazy old conglomerates there, reposing in awful cliffs and massive columns on the mountain's side; and here, let us "calmly" survey the harvests fields, the fresh-mown hay, the little white cottages looking like children's playthings, scattered over the valley "away down below." How beautiful, in this tremendous ocean of untamed and unchiseled mountains, the little narrow patches of the farmer appear! They look like long pieces of richly figured carpet, while the stately pines give them a border of the darkest and softest green. Rising one after the other, like an army of soldiers, to the mountain top, their tall spear-shaped plumes pierce the region of clouds, while beneath they bury their quivering shadows in the solemn depths of solitude; for

> The sound of the church-going bell
>   These valleys and rocks ne'er heard,—
> Ne'er sighed at the sound of a knell,
>   Or smiled when a Sabbath appeared.

At the terminus of the railroad flows the Lehigh river, a stream of no great volume, except in times of long continued rain. At such seasons the banks are overflowed, and some of the villages and property on its banks occasionally suffer material injury. The banks are deep and much worn in consequence of the velocity of the stream, and the large amount of debris collected in the mountains are carried down in the current. The Lehigh empties into the Delaware river at Easton, a distance of thirty-six miles from Mauch Chunk. It is made

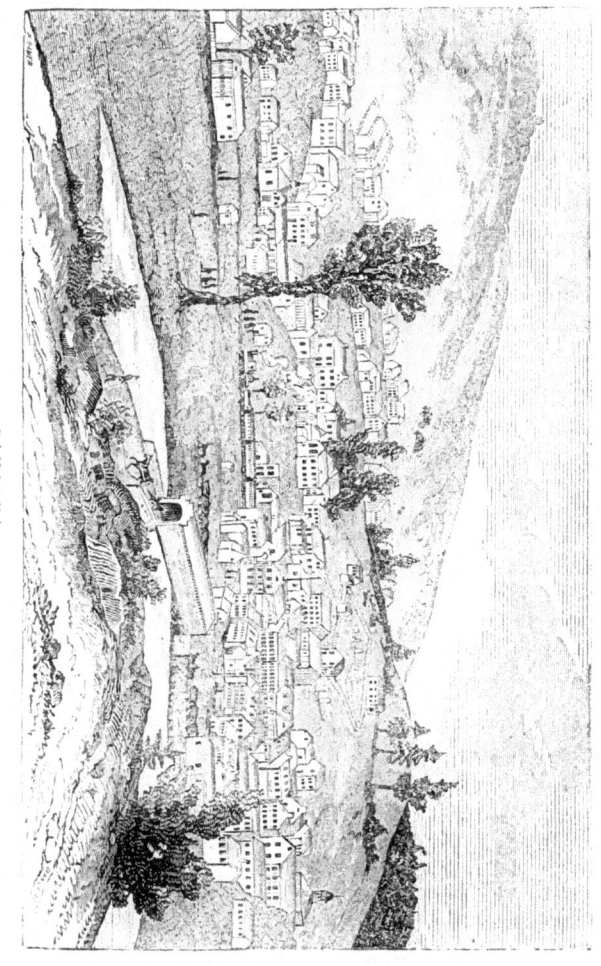
TAMAQUA.

navigable to Easton, and also to White Haven, twenty-six miles above, for coal boats of one hundred tons. Beyond White Haven to Stoddartsville, the river has been improved for descending lumber, which forms a large trade on this river, besides that of coal. The Lehigh Coal and Navigation Company, under whose auspices these stupendous improvements were made, own upwards of ten thousand acres of the coal land embraced in this region, while their works afford an outlet for the adjacent coal districts of Beaver Meadow, Spring Mountain, Hazleton, Buck Mountain, White Haven, etc. Projects for the navigation of the Lehigh were set on foot as early as 1792; but it was only after the discovery of coal, and when its importance began to be righly appreciated, that its entire completion was effected. A vast amount of capital has been sunk unnecessarily, which has involved the present company to a serious extent; but the growing importance of its trade must and will ultimately place the works in a paying condition.

To effect the transfer of coal from the cars to the canal boats, extensive steam and other works are employed. In the first place, there is an inclined plane, running from the railroad, (which terminates at a point about one hundred and fifty feet above the level of the river), to the banks of the canal-basin, where tressel-works are erected, projecting over the river. Over this plane the loaded cars descend. The rapidity of their descent is in a measure checked by the weight of the empty cars ascending, which, being fastened at the other end of the rope, and moving on a parallel railway on the same plane, necessarily mount as rapidly as the loaded cars descend. But the partial counterpoise is still insufficient to moderate properly the speed of the descending cars. This object is effectually gained by an iron band which clasps the drum, (to which the rope is attached,) and which, compressed by a lever, controls its motion. Accidents have rarely occurred in this descent, but the cars have sometimes deviated or broken loose. They are now guarded against by a very simple, yet ingenious contrivance. The railway is double until the most rapid part of the descent is passed, when both ways curve and unite into one. Should a car break loose, therefore, its momentum will be so great as to prevent its following the curve, and as soon as it reaches the spot, it is thrown off the track, overturned, and lodged on a clay bank formed for this purpose below. Farther down, a bulwark is constructed, over-arching the railway, to intercept the loose coal as it flies from the cars. When the car arrives at the foot of the inclined plane, it pitches into a downward curve in the railway, and a projecting bar, which secures the lower end of the car, and which, for this purpose, is hung in a horizontal axis, knocks it open, and the coal slides down a steep funnel or shute, into the canal boat, which, receding from the shore by the impulse thus given it, occasions the coal to spread evenly over its bottom.

In addition to this inclined plane, however, there are shutes connecting directly with the railroad and the banks of the canal. These shutes are probably upwards of two hundred feet in length, lined with an iron flooring. The coal is thrown in from the car above, and slides down to the boats in the canal, thus saving the trouble and expense of hoisting the cars up and down. These works are all indicated in the engraving annexed.

After the cars are unloaded, they are returned to the summit, in precisely the same manner as they came down—that is, by gravitation. To effect this, two inclined planes are used, one of which, on the top of Mount Pisgah, is indicated in the engraving. A stationary steam-engine is placed at the head of each plane, by means of which the empty cars are drawn up. After reaching the top of Mount Pisgah, they descend by gravitation a distance of six miles, when the other plane is reached. Raised over this, they descend again, in like manner, until they get their supplies of coal, when they are returned on the road already described. An imaginary railway circle is thus described, over which the cars proceed with the swiftness, almost, of lightning, without any motive-power whatever. Mount Pisgah plane is twenty-two hundred and fifty feet in length, overcoming a perpendicular height of nearly seven hundred feet. This is probably the greatest elevation overcome by any other single inclined plane in the world. Previous to the completion of this new road, the empty cars were drawn back by mules, that always accompanied the loaded trains in their descent, having had cars expressly appropriated to their accommodation. Upwards of six hundred mules were thus employed, occasioning, as may well be supposed, a heavy item of expense, including that necessary for the support of their drivers. It is, in our opinion, a serious obstacle to the success of this company, that so much machinery, and that of an expensive and complicated character, has to be maintained to carry on their business.

MAUCH CHUNK is a remarkable village, and no engraving could hope

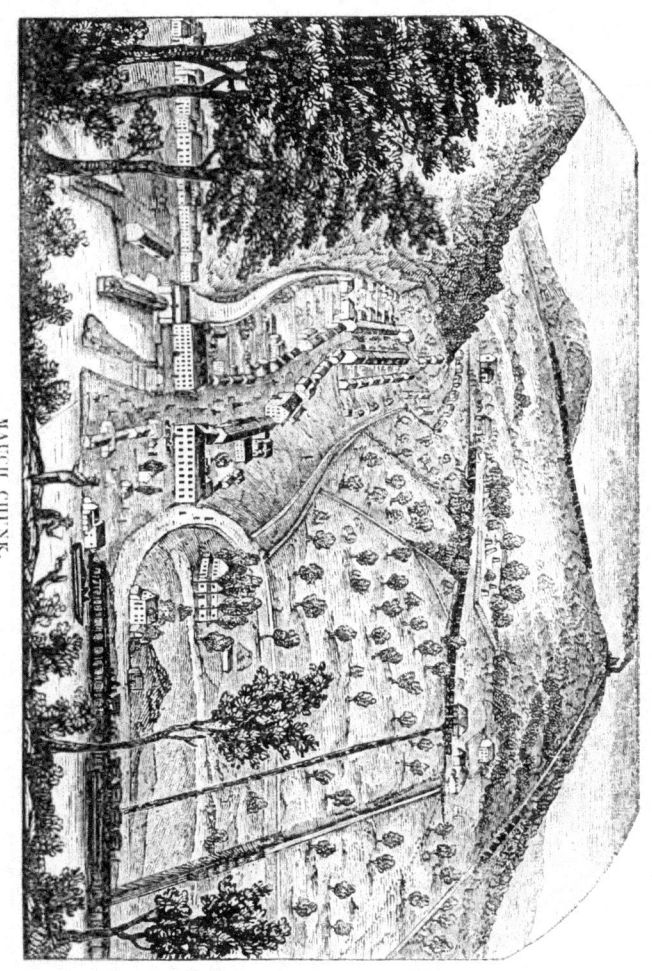

MAUCH CHUNK.

to portray its peculiar features—nor, indeed, could any considerable portion of it, small as it is, be exhibited in a single view, since the town creeps in amongst the narrow valleys of the numerous mountains, in which it is situated, for nestling places. It is a bird's-nest of a place—hemmed in by high and steep mountains on all sides—some gracefully curving around it, while others terminate abruptly in its midst, and seemingly frown down upon it. The houses, which are generally very neat and creditable structures, are built on the sides of the mountains—in some instances the fronts presenting three and four stories, the rear *one*. There are two principal hotels, which are much frequented during the summer months by travellers and tourists, but more especially by enterprizing capitalists and manufacturers interested in the vast resources of the country, and who, being usually accompanied by their wives and daughters, make their visit one of business as well as pleasure—mingling profit with the pursuit of novelty and entertainment—wild scenery, wholesome air, and so forth.

We have now—oh, reader!—we have now finished Part First of this, our "Travels!"

PART II.

The Anthracite Coal Formation.

"I will teach you to pierce the bowels of the earth, and bring out from the caverns of mountains metals which will give strength to our hands, and subject all nature to our use and pleasure."—*Dr. Johnson.*

COAL is indisputably a *vegetable production*, and occupies a position low down, among the earliest deposits of the primeval earth. For a long time it was hard to recognize its vegetable origin, because the fact opened the door to some of the grandest and most wonderful phenomena ever grasped by philosophy—originating theories and hypotheses, as it did, which conflicted not only with every previous opinion, but seemingly struck a heavy blow at the truths of revealed law. Instead of the earth being but a few thousand years old, the coal deposits prove it to be of great and incalculable antiquity—numbering its years not by centuries, but rather by thousands and millions far anterior to the flood. Nor is its wonderful antiquity inconsistent, as was at first supposed, with the doctrines of divine revelation.* Science and Religion are identical in their true mission,

---

* Prof. Silliman, during a recent course of lectures on Geology, before the Smithsonian Institute at Washington, stated, decidedly, that there is no conflict between geology and the scripture history. The case is widely different from that of astronomy, more than two hundred years ago, which was condemned as heretical, because the scriptures described the *appearances* of the heavens only, which were all that in general mankind could be acquainted with.

But in the case of geology, there is not even a literal discrepancy. On the contrary, all the geological formations correspond in the order of time, and, as far as they are described in the scriptures, with the nature of the deposits, and cannot fail to harmonize when properly understood. The beneficent doctrines of the great Mediator were promulgated at a period when the world was unprepared either for the startling truths or the practical benefits of science—hence it was left for the Bible to *gradually*

especially in the succession of created beings endowed with life, and man in both systems crowns the whole.

The only change required is extension of time, so as to afford enough to allow the events to happen by natural laws, established by the Creator, and expressive of his will, which is thus distinctly recorded in the earth itself. "The beginning" is not limited in time, and may extend as far back as the case may require; thus providing for all the early formations.

The periods called days are not necessarily such as we now denote by that word. There could be no regulation and division of time, as we now have it, until the sun was set to rule the day. Morning and evening may be, before that time, figurative expressions, denoting merely beginning and ending, as we say the morning and evening of life. The word day is used, in this short narrative, in all the senses in which it is ever employed in language, and significantly in the recapitulation or summary; in the beginning of the second chapter, day is used for the whole period of the creation, and in the same sense in various other parts of the scriptures.

The periods required for all the amazing series of events recorded in the earth are necessarily long; and if time was measured by natural days in the fifth and sixth periods, during the creation and sepulture of innumerable races of marine and terrestrial animals, there must have been a repetition of very many of those days to make out a long epoch, which might as well be regarded at once as a period of sufficient length for the work.

The Sabbath stands by itself, after the work is finished, a moral institution, having no necessary connection with the preceding physical events. By it man is every week reminded of his Maker and his destination, and although neither morning nor evening are in the Genesis named in connection with the Sabbath, it has no doubt always been of the same length as now, and does not belong to the geological epochs.

If this view is not acceptable, it is still indispensable, that in some way the time should be found, and no person fully acquainted with the structure of the earth can doubt that the time was very long, and no other person can be admitted as qualified to judge in the case. There is no reason to believe that man has been in the world more than six thousand years and the antiquity of the planet refers to ages before man was created. The allusion in the commandments, and in other parts of the scriptures, to the six days would of course be made in conformity with the language adopted in the narrative, which, being for the mass of mankind, was necessarily a popular history, although of divine origin; and the historian adopted a division of time that was in general use, *prepare* and guide fallen man to a higher and nobler destiny, rather than to confound and corrupt him with a premature and *unnatural* perception of the mysteries of the universe, and the great social and physical laws that impel him onward. This is the mission of the although as to half the time, at least, it was inconsistent with astronomical laws. Extension of the time to such a length as to cover the events by the operation of physical laws removes every difficulty, interferes with no doctrine of religion, and prepares us to exclaim with our divine poets—

> These are thy glorious works, Parent of Good:
> Almighty! thine this universal frame,
> Thus wondrous fair: Thyself how wondrous, then,
> Unspeakable, who sits above the heavens,
> To us invisible, or dimly seen in these thy lower works.
> Yet these declare thy goodness beyond thought,
> And power divine.—*Milton.*

> Thou giv'st its lustre to an insect's wing,
> And wheel'st thy throne upon the rolling worlds.
> From Thee is all that cheers the life of man,
> His high endeavour and his glad success—
> His power to suffer and his will to serve;
> But oh! Thou bounteous Giver of all good,
> Thou art of all thy gifts thyself the crown.
> Give what thou canst; without Thee we are poor—
> And with Thee rich, take what thou wilt away.—*Cowper.*

Bayard Taylor who, at the last advices received from him, was in Egypt, gives the following in connection with his visit to the great temple of Abou-Simbel. "The sculptures on the walls of the grand hall are, after those of Medeenet Abou, and on the exterior wall of Karnak, the most interesting I have seen in Egypt. On the end wall, on either side of the entrance, is a colossal bas-relief, representing Remeses slaying a group of captive kings, whom he holds by the hair of their heads. There are ten or twelve in each group, and the features, though they are not coloured, exhibit the same distinction of race as I had previously remarked in Belzoni's tomb, at Thebes. There is the Negro, the Persian, the Jew, and one other form of countenance which I could not make out—all imploring with uplifted hands the mercy of the conqueror. On the southern wall, the distinction between the Negro and the Egyptian is made still more obvious by the coloring of the figures. In fact, I see no reason whatever to doubt that the peculiar characteristics of the different races of men were as strongly marked in the days of Remeses as at present. This is an interesting fact in discussing the question of the unity of origin of the races. I

Bible, and wherever its pages have been freely unfolded, there has science followed, and proclaimed her unyielding laws.

Referring the primary origin of the earth itself to the nebular theory of Herschell, it is supposed to be filled with everlasting fire—the result, probably, of its internal chemical organization, or the original incandescence of the planet. However this may be, the existence of universal heat within it, is amply demonstrated by the variation of the temperature of the atmosphere as we proceed downwards—a descent of a few thousand feet bringing us into a region entirely too warm to sustain life. It is further demonstrated by volcanic eruptions, which have through all time, and at various places, vomited out streams of burning lava and scoriæ, overflowing vast regions of country, as well as filling up the bottoms of the sea; while in more recent times they have buried entire cities—men, women, and children; servant and master; resident and stranger; the princely palace—the capitol—the column, and the arch—all buried in one common grave! To such eruptions, as the inevitable consequence of inextinguishable fire, should also be added the phenomenon of earthquakes, which are no less disastrous and terrible in their effects, and no less frequent in their visits. These elements of destruction have probably been awakened at irregular periods, and when fully aroused, have operated generally throughout the globe, rather than in isolated districts; hence gradually arose the vast mountain chains that now traverse the face of the globe, from pole to pole, throwing back, in their ascent, the waters of the sea, and dividing them by impenetrable barriers. Thus was slowly produced a material refrigeration of the climate—for it must be understood that, previous to these epochs, the climate of the earth must have been universal, or nearly so, and that, at least, it was much warmer than it now is, even in the torrid zone. This is evident from the fact that coal is distributed in all quarters of the globe—in cold as well as in warm regions.

have as yet, though deeply interested in the subject, not looked into it sufficiently to take either side; but, admitting the different races of men to have had originally one origin, the date of the first appearance of Man on the earth, must have been nearer fifty thousand than five thousand years ago. If climate, customs, and the like, have been the only agents in producing that variety of race, which we find so strongly marked nearly four thousand years ago, surely those agents must have been at work for a vastly longer period than that usually accepted as the age of Man. We are older than we know; but our beginning, like our end, is darkness and mystery.

Whatever may have been the local characteristics of the primeval earth, it is certain that the climate was much warmer, and much more humid than it now is, or has been in modern times. The character of the vegetation abundantly establishes this. Of the large number of plants comprising the coal-bearing period, there are few which bear any analogy to existing species, and these are the exclusive productions of the torrid zone. Fossil Botany, it is true, is a comparatively recent science—yet enough has been elicited through its aid to afford a good idea of the vegetation of the ancient earth. The vegetation of the coal formation, according to Dr. Lindley, consisted of ferns in vast abundance; of large coniferous trees, of species resembling *lycopodiaceæ*, but of most gigantic dimensions; of vast quantities of a tribe apparently analagous to *cacteæ* or *euphorbiaceæ*, but perhaps not identical with them; of palms and other monocotyledous; and, finally, of numerous plants, the exact nature of which is doubtful. Of the entire number of species detected in this formation, two-thirds are ferns. The fossils are divided by Botanists into the following genera, determined by the character of their fronds; pachypteris, sphenopteris, cyclopteris, glossopteris, neuropteris, odontopteris, anomopteris, tæaniopteris, pecopteris, louchopteris, clathropteris, schizopteris, otopteris, caulopteris and sigillaria, etc., the two latter occurring only as stems, and the last being considered by many as a dicotyledonous plant. Of these, figure 1 exhibits a specimen of the neuropteris, or

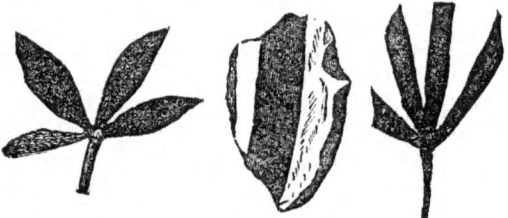

FIG. 1.—NEUROPTERIS.

nerve fern, which are plentifully distributed in the coal. Figure 2 is a specimen of the odontopteris, or tooth-fern, not so numerous as the former, but still characteristic of this formation. The next, Anomopteris, are seldom met with, but nevertheless flourished in this era.

FIG. 2. ODONTOPTERIS.   FIG. 3.—ANOMOPTERIS.

The Pecopteris, figure 4, is by far the most numerous of all varieties of the fern, having upwards of sixty different species in the coal. The common brake, or fern, exhibits a type of the family of which the figure will serve as a specimen; but the arborescent ferns, which now grow only in the vicinity of the equator, present the closest analogy to those of the carboniferous period, which were lofty trees, far surpassing in height and magnificence, even their tropical congeners of the present day. From their number and variety, they afford some of the most interesting fossil remains which the vegetable kingdom has produced. Their leaves are generally elegant, and display great variety of form and diversity of venation; from these characters the generic and specific distinctions of the family are obtained. They are often preserved in great perfection, and even the organs of fructification are occasionally observable at the back of the leaf. Several fine specimens of the fern may be seen at the Pennsylvania Hall, in Pottsville, while nearly every coal operator has more or less of various kinds of vegetable fossil, which they exhibit for the gratification of friends. Martin Weaver, Esq., has shown us several of the finest impressions we have yet seen, and he had, at one time, if he has not now, a considerable collection.

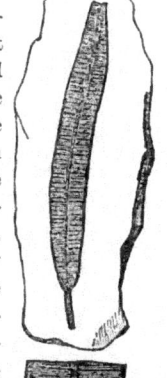

Fig. 4.—Pecopteris.

11*

Fig. 5 exhibits a variety of fruit, of the family of *Chara*, and comprised in the same class as the foregoing. The fruit is oval, and consists of five valves, twisted spirally, with a small opening at each extremity. The figure on the left, marked 1, exhibits the nut within

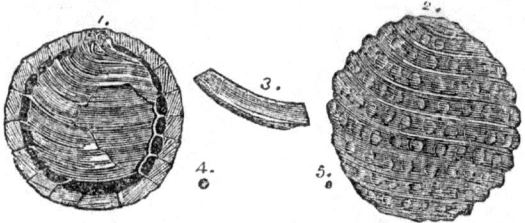

FIG. 5.—CHARA.

the pericarp; 2 shows the pericarp; and 3 a portion of the spiral valve, magnified, while 4 and 5 are the natural size of 1 and 2, magnified in the engraving. Of the family of the *club-moss* or *lycopodiaceæ*, there are numerous specimens, the most common of which are the lycopadites, lepidodendron, lepidostrobus, and stigmaria, a specimen of which we append—fig. 6. The stem of the Stigmaria was

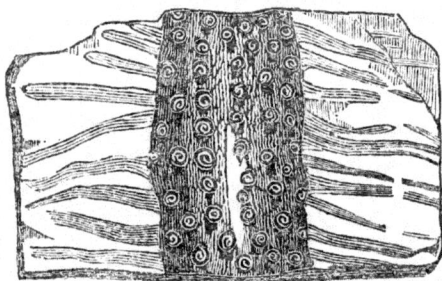

FIG. 6.—STIGMARIA.

originally succulent, marked externally with roundish tubercles, surrounded by a groove, and arranged in a direction more or less spiral —having a distinct axis, communicating with the tubercles by woody processes. Fig. 7 exhibits a specimen of the Pterophyllum, or wingleaf, of the family of *Cycadeæ*, seldom met with in the coal, and of which the leaves only are known. Fig. 8, however, of the same family, called *Asterophyllites*, is one of the most numerous dicotyle-

ANTHRACITE COAL FORMATION. 127

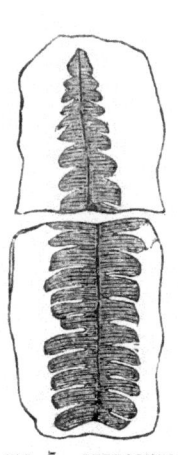

FIG. 7.—PTEROPHYLLUM.   FIG. 8.—ASTERAPHYLLITES.

donous plants found in the coal, but unlike the other, the *stems* only are known. There is a variety of others which it is probably unnecessary to specify—the examples already afforded being, we think, quite sufficient to convey an idea of the several families comprising the coal vegetation. Of the numerous families composing the class of monocotyledonous plants, there are comparatively few to be found in the coal formation. The class of dicotyledonous, however, presents a greater variety and number, most of which belong to the family

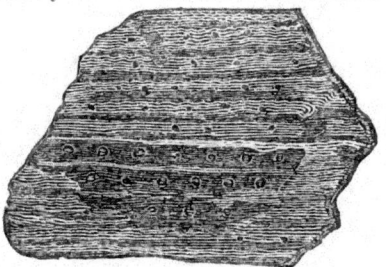

FIG. 9.—SIGILLARIA.

of *Sigillaria*, of which fig. 9 affords a specimen. The Sigillaria is one of the most important plants of the coal, and probably furnished a very large amount of its vegetable matter. The stem is conical, and deeply furrowed, with scars between the furrows in rows, but not arranged in a distinctly spiral manner. There are some forty species in the coal formation.

The most common of the coal-plants may be classified as follows: first, ferns and Sigillaria. Second, lepidodendron, a doubtful genus, variously associated by botanists. Thirdly, calamites. Fourthly, coniferous plants; and fifthly, stigmaria, which is probably an extinct family. To ascertain more satisfactorily the nature and circumstances attending the growth of the vegetable matter, it is necessary to institute some further inquiries. Thus, by comparisons with *existing species*, and the elements constituting their growth, we obtain considerable light on the subject, and are able to form conclusions which could not otherwise be safely arrived at. We shall append a few illustrations. The Sigillaria, so numerous in the coal, have generally been classed as monocotyledonous plants; but late observers contend that they properly belong to the dicotyledonous division. The irregular and longitudinal furrows of the surface of the stems —their swelling out at the base, angle of dip or downward direction of the roots, are characters constantly observable in the dicotyledonous, but never in monocotyledonous plants. Besides, these trees have a separable bark; and slices of it, prepared for microscopic investigation, have exhibited traces of medullary rays, which are universally recognized as proofs of dicotyledonous structure. While they are

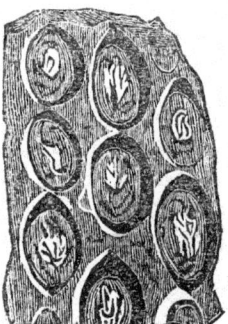 

FIG. 10.—CAULOPTERIS.   FIG. 11.—EXISTING TREE-FERN.

thus regarded as dicotyledonous, or exogenous and compact trees, Dr. Lindley has divided from them another genus, termed *caulopteris*,

ANTHRACITE COAL FORMATION.   129

which he considers true stems of tree-ferns. These are hollow, but the markings which they exhibit present so close a resemblance to existing tree-ferns as to leave no doubt of their identity with those plants. They are, however, comparatively rare in the coal; while of the true Sigillaria, over forty species have been discovered. We append a figure of the fossil stem, caulopteris, 10, and a figure of an existing tree-fern, 11, in juxtaposition for comparison.

The family of Lepidodendra have, by some writers, been supposed to belong to that of the club-mosses; while the larger species were regarded as forming a transition to the coniferous plants. The living species of their supposed analogues, fig. 12, abound in tropical climates;—they generally creep on the ground, some grow erect, but none exceed three feet in height; whereas, fossil specimens have been found over thirty feet high, while fragments have been discovered

FIG. 12.—CLUB-MOSS.

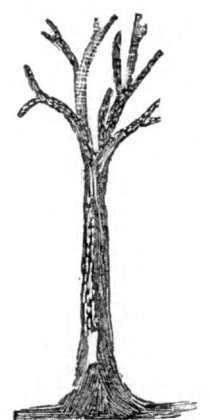
FIG. 13.—LEPIDODENDRA.

indicating a much larger size, figs. 13 and 14. Figure 15 exhibits a specimen of a numerous family, called *Crassula Tetragona*, probably allied to the above species, which are found at the Cape of Good Hope. They occur in the driest situations, where not a blade of grass nor a particle of moss can grow, on naked rocks, old walls, or hot sandy plains, alternately exposed to the heaviest dews of night, and the most intense rays of the noon-day sun. Soil is to them a something to keep them stationary, rather than a source of nutriment,

R

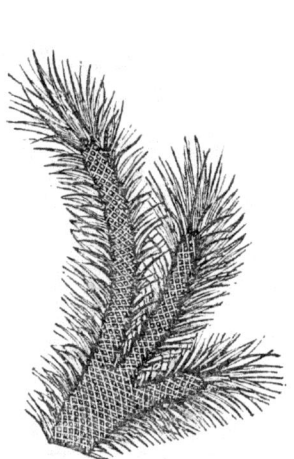

FIG. 14.—LEPIDODIA.   FIG. 15.—CRASSULA TETRAGONA.

which, in these plants, is conveyed in myriads of small cuticular pores, to the cellular tissue which lies beneath them.

The Calamites are not analogous to any existing species, as already noted, though they resemble some plants in structure, but differ widely in their proportions—the fossil indicating large trees, while the existing species which they resemble are but two or three feet high, and of corresponding diameter. Of the coniferæ of the coal, it has been observed that they bear a strong resemblance to existing *pines*—slices of the wood, when examined by the microscope, showing that the ducts or glands peculiar to this family of trees, are arranged in a similar manner, that is, alternately in double and triple rows, fig. 16.

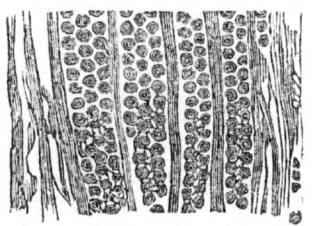

FIG. 16.—CONIFERÆ.

The stigmaria is generally supposed to have been a large succulent water-plant—the stem, in its compressed fossil state, varying from two to six inches in diameter, and has numerous processes, which proceed vertically, horizontally and obliquely, and traverse the beds in every direction. These processes have been traced to a distance of eight or ten feet from the stem, and had a horizontal range of twenty feet. From the extraordinary number of these plants, it is concluded that they have furnished the material for the great bulk of our coal beds.

From the general character of the vegetation, and the absence of the great mountain ranges which now conspicuously mark the earth's surface, it is probable that water covered a far greater area of country than it subsequently did, while, at the same time, its mineral qualities must have been essentially different from what they are now.

FIG. 17.—THE COAL VEGETATION.

The land, lying low and in broad marshes, must have resembled, in some respects, our great western prairies, so well known for their rank vegetation, which, added to the peculiar warmth and humidity of the climate, produced plants of extraordinary proportions—far exceeding our loftiest forest trees. The vegetable matter growing thus spontaneously under active stimulants, formed immense wild coverings, by which it was peculiarly adapted to receive the ascending charges of the elements constituting its growth. Fig. 17 exhibits an ideal view of the coal vegetation.

Regarding the manner of deposit, much difference of opinion exists among Geologists. For a long time an opinion prevailed (and is still entertained by some), that the vegetable matter was removed from the place of its growth by drift, and deposited in the bottom of the sea, or the estuaries of lakes and rivers, where it underwent a process of fermentation and pressure from the superimposed debris that accumulated upon it, and thus gradually changed into the state of coal. It is now, however, rendered probable that it grew on the identical beds in which we find it, and the supposition is supported from the fact, amongst others, that fossil trees have been found in the coal formation in an erect position, with portions of their trunks charred, and passing into the state of coal, which is, of course, inconsistent with the theory of their removal by drift.

Indeed, when we consider the enormous amount of vegetable matter entering into, and necessary to have produced even the smallest seam of coal, it is hard to conceive how it could have drifted from the place of growth—especially, too, as the floating mass would have been exposed to the liability of meeting and intermixing with various other substances, tending to impair the purity of the coal; whereas no such evidence is afforded. It is obvious, therefore, that the coal grew on the spots where it is now deposited, and the only remaining point to establish this view, is to account for the deposition of the *intermediate strata*. This, however, is not an easy task—for they comprise marine deposits of every description, in addition to those of sand, clay, and mud, which have produced the extensive sandstone rock that lies around the seams of coal. The only way it can be accounted for, is to suppose the submergence of the coal beds, time after time, and the deposition of the sea-shells and crustaceæ, that are now found over them, combined with the conglomerate detritris borne into the estuaries of lakes and rivers—after which the waters probably receded, and suffered another supply of vegetable matter to accumulate. That something like this process is at least probable, is sufficiently evident from the alternation of marine deposits and other matter with the coal beds, and their position high up upon the summits of mountains, hundreds of miles from the present flow of the sea. How else could they have been deposited there, in regular order and succession?—though it is nevertheless probable that extraordinary floods, internal convulsions and outbreaks in the earth's crust, as well as the general changes of land into sea, and sea into land, at that period, (and even now constantly going on,) contributed much as co-operative agents. We append a single figure, 18, showing the horizontal position of strata, which will also serve to illustrate the alternation of coal veins with other deposits in the same basins.

FIGURE 18.

The vegetable material, therefore, having been thus secured, a chemical process subsequently ensued, as before stated, by which the mass was turned into coal. The fermentation produced by the pressure of the overlaying strata, and the impossibility of the immediate escape of its gaseous elements, heated it sufficiently to produce a body of pitchy or bituminous matter, and the coal is consequently bituminous, or only partially so, in proportion as these gases were subsequently let out by the cracks, and fissures, and disruptions, going on in the surrounding strata. For we find that when the strata are undisturbed, bituminous or fat coals predominate; whereas, where the strata are inverted, and torn and disruptured, anthracite, or coals which have lost the greater portion of this pitchy matter, prevail. Thus, after long-continued and constantly increasing pressure, the vegetable matter becomes one compact body of coal; and now, after the lapse of countless centuries, during which the process of mineralization has still continued, we find it embracing every shade and variety of quality, according to the original ingredients constituting the growth, age, and local circumstances governing its deposition.

In connection with this branch of the subject, we present the following extracts from the opinions of Sir Charles Lyell, of England, who visited this region in 1841. In reference to the origin of coal, whatever dispute there may have been on the subject, he thinks was settled when a portion of the New Castle coal, some years ago, was submitted to a *microscopic examination*. After cutting off a slice so thin that it should transmit light, it was found that many parts of the pure and solid coal, in which geologists had no suspicion that they should be able to deduct any vegetable structures, not only were the annular rings of the growth of several kinds of trees beautifully distinct, but even the medullary rays, and what is still more remarkable, in some cases, even the spiral vessels could be discovered. But besides these proofs, from observing a vegetable structure in the coal itself, there has been found in the shales accompanying it, fern leaves and branches, as well as other plants, and when we find the trunks of trees and bark converted into this same kind of coal as we find in the great solid beds, no one will dispute the strong evidence in favor of the vegetable origin of this coal. If we find a circumference of bark surrounding a cylindrical mass of sand, we know that it has been a hollow tree filled up with sand, nor can there be any doubt that the coal is formed of vegetable matter. No less than three hundred species of plants have been well determined by botanists; some of whom have devoted a great part of their lives to this study. From this it is to be inferred that the carboniferous formation of Europe and America is made up of comparatively recent plants. He thus alludes to three or four of the most peculiar facts which lead to this conclusion.

In the first place, the boughs and leaves of ferns are the most frequently and strikingly met in America as well as Europe. So perfectly have they been preserved that there can be no doubt that they are really ferns; and in some cases even their infloresence has been preserved at the back of the leaves. Where we have not the flowers and prints remaining we have found it possible to distinguish the different species of fossil and ancient ferns by attending to the veining of the leaves. At least one hundred species are determined in this way. The most numerous of those vegetable veinings are those which have been called *Sigillaria or tree ferns*. Their stems are found to be fluted vertically, and in the flutings are little stars, as it were, each of which indicates the place where the leaf was attached; and it is evident, as M. Brongniart has shown, that although the bark of these trees is so well marked that forty-two species have been described, yet there is never found any leaf attached; while we have in the same beds leaves in abundance which have no trunks. The natural inference is, that they must have belonged to the aborescent ferns; as, for instance, the section *Cauloptoris* is admitted by all to have belonged to this species. The fact is also important because the tree-ferns, and especially the *Cauloptoris*, are now known to be exclusively the inhabitants of a *warm and humid climate*—much more hot and moist than in those parts of the globe where coal now abounds. For we find coal, not only in England and Nova Scotia, but as far north as Melville's Island and Baffin's Bay, in a climate where the growth of such fern plants is dwarfish and stinted. It is evident that when these vegetables existed there must have been a warmer, and probably a more equable climate than is now found even in warmer latitudes.

The climate in Northern latitudes was then much warmer and more moist than it is now in any part of the globe. The same thing is made evident by a comparison of their fossil *Sigillaria* with those which now attain their greatest size in the islands of the Pacific. He had found several plants, as the *Asterophyllites*, in the Apalachian Chain, and which are also found] in Nova Scotia and Europe, which cannot certainly be referred to any living families. These all, however, bespeak a terrestrial vegetation, though occasionally found mixed with marine shells and corals.

Another class of fossils common in coal shales is the *Lepidodendra*, somewhat allied in form to the modern *Licopodiums*, or white mosses. Though the mosses of the present day are never more than shrubs, even in the warmest regions, yet, at the carboniferous period they attained an enormous development, being forty, fifty, or even seventy feet high.

There have been two theories to explain how these plants could have been carried into the sea, estuaries, or lakes, and drawn beneath the water and accumulated in the strata, so as to form coal. One of them asserts that the plants must have been drifted and buried in the water, since we find them intercollated between different strata of shales; just as plants lie between the leaves of a botanist's *herbarium*, and are pressed together, so have these ferns been found flattened between the seams of shale. They have been carried from the place where they grew, drifted out to a certain distance, water-logged and sunk in the mud, and other strata deposited above them, so as to form this intercollation between the different leaves of clay.

But many believed, from seeing the roots, that the plants grew on the spot where we now find them. But when we come to observe that these roots terminate in different strata, it will seem evident that they were carried down, sunk and struck in the mud, as snags are now in the Mississippi. * * * * This may appear contradictory to what has been said with regard to a change of climate since the carboniferous era; but it is not necessarily so. The opinion of Werner, confirmed by the speculations of Brongniart, led him to believe, contrary to his early impressions, that by far the greater part of the coal had grown on the spot where it is found. Accumulating like peat in the land, the land must have been submerged again and again, to allow the strata of sand and mud to be superimposed as we now find them.

In excavating for coal at Belgray, near Glasgow, in 1835, many upright trees were found with their roots terminating in a bed of coal; and only seven years ago, in cutting a section of the Bolton Railroad in Lancashire, eight or ten trees were found in a vertical position; they were referrable to the *Lipidodendra* species, and allied *Licopidiums*, or club mosses. All were within forty or fifty feet of each other, and some of them were fifteen feet in circumference at the bottom. The roots spread in all directions, and reached beds of clay, and also spread out into the seams of coal. There is no doubt that these trees grew where they are found, and that the roots are in their original position. The seam of coal has possibly been formed of the leaves which fell from the trees. This is a singular fact: that just below the coal seam, and above the covering of the roots, was found more than a bushel of the *Lepidostrobus*—a fruit not unlike the elongated cone of the fir tree. It has always been imagined that the *Lepidostrabus* was the fruit of the *Lepidodendra*, but here they are found beneath other trees.

Under every seam of coal in Wales is found the fire-clay—a sandy, blue mud, abounding in the plants called *Stigmaria.* First is the seam of coal, then the fire-clay, then another seam of coal, and then the sandstone. In one open part of the Newcastle coal field, about thirty species of *Sigillariæ* were discovered: the trunks were two or three feet in diameter. They pierce through the sand in a vertical direction, and after going for some eleven feet perpendicularly, the upper part bends round horizontally, and extends laterally into the sand—and then they are so flattened by the superincumbent strata, that the opposite barks are forced within half an inch of each other. The flutings are beautifully preserved in the flattened horizontal stems. Here had been an ancient forest growing in a bed of clay—buried in some way with sand to a certain depth, and then the upper part was bent and broken off by the water current, and buried in layers of shale and mud. There are many cases of this kind in Wales, where the roots of the trees evidently preserve their original position. Mr. Logan, an excellent geologist, has examined no less than ninety of these seams of coal in Wales. They are so exceedingly thin that they are but of little value in an economical light—yet, they are just as important for geological purposes, as if they were thick strata. Under every one of the ninety, he has found fire-clay, a sandy mud, containing the plants called *Stigmaria.* It was discovered years ago that this fire-clay existed with the coal mine; but it was not known that it was the floor of every coal seam, and not the root, which contained this plant in a perfect state. The *Stigmaria* appears in the under-clay (to use the term employed by the miners,) a cylindrical stem, from every side of which extends leaves—not only from the opposite sides, but from every side, they appear like tubercles, fitting on as by a joint. They radiate in all directions in the mud, where they are not flattened like the ferns. Had they been, we might have had leaves in two directions, but not on every side. These plants resemble the *Euphorbiaceæ* in their structure, and in some respects are analogous to the caniferous or fir tribes. In their whole structure, they are distinct from all living genera or families of plants. In one instance, a dome-shaped mass was found with stems and leaves—some of the branches being twenty or thirty feet in length, and sometimes longer. It has been thought by Dr. Buckland and other geologists, that those plants either trailed along in the mud at the bottom of the swamps, or floated in lakes like the modern *Stratiotes.*

After Mr. Logan had arrived at this remarkable fact, Mr. Lyell became particularly desirous to know if the same fact was true in the United States. When he arrived here in August, 1841, he had no idea how far it was true, yet it was known the *Stigmaria* did occur; and his first opportunity to inquire into the fact was at Blossburg, in the Bituminous field, in the northern part of this state. His first inquiry of the geologist was, whether he found *Stigmaria* there. He received in answer an affirmative reply; and on being asked if the plant occurred in the *under-clay,* he said that they could soon settle the point. Whereupon he had one of the mines lighted up, and the only plant *they could find in the under-clay was this Stigmaria.* It existed in abundance—its leaves radiating in all directions, just as in Wales, more than four thousand miles distant. The same cretal appearance was preserved. In the roof of the coal seam were seen different species of ferns—*Sigillaria* and *Calamites*, just as in North Carolina and in Wales. Afterwards another opportunity occurred in the Pottsville region of anthracite coal. Professor Rodgers, the state geologist, who, though well acquainted with the strata of the district, was as anxious as Mr. Lyell to know if the rule would hold good, examined, first at Pottsville, and then at Mauch Chunk, and the same phenomenon was observed at both points. In the first coal mine they came to, the coal had all been quarried away (for the work was carried on in open day), and nothing but the cheeks of the mine remained. The beds, as they have been horizontal, are now not vertical, but have gone through an angle of little more than ninety degrees, and turned a little over, so that what is now the under side was originally the upper; therefore, the cheek on the left side was originally the floor of the mine. They now looked at the lower cheek, and the first thing they saw was the *Stigmaria*, very distinct; on the other side, but a little way off were Ferns, Sigillaria, Calamites, Asterophyllites, but no *Stigmaria*. So it was at Mauch Chunk, where they found one thirty feet long, with leaves radiating in all directions.

It has now been ascertained for many years that Professor Caton was quite correct in affirming the anthracite and bituminous coals to be of the same age. This is shown, not only by their relative position with regard to the red sandstone, but from the plants found in both being identical.

All the coal fields, therefore, may be regarded as one whole, and the question will occur, how did it happen that the great floor was let down so as to prevent the accumulation of coal, and yet plants of so different textures should be found in it. It has been suggested that these plants grew in the swamps; and it is possible to imagine that there may have been morasses fitted only for the growth of the species of plants called *Stigmaria;* and that, as this marsh filled up, this and the other plants became dry, and the leaves accumulated one layer above another, so as to form beds of coal of a different nature from those that preceded. We know it is a common thing for shallow ponds to fill up gradually with mud and aquatic plants, and at last peat and trees are formed upon them. A corresponding change is constantly going on in different parts of Europe—the same transition from bogs and marshes to a soil capable of supporting various great trees is taking place, and then the ground is submerged; for always, again and again, we must refer to this subsidence of the soil.

Those who have seen the morass called the Great Dismal in North Carolina and Virginia, may possibly have had an opportunity of crossing the northern extremity of it on a railway supported by piles, from Norfolk to Welden. There is no less than forty miles from North to South, and twenty from East to West, covered entirely with various forest trees, under which is a great quantity of moss; the vegetation is of every variety of size, from common creeping moss to tall cypresses one hundred and thirty feet high. The water surrounds the roots of these trees for many months in the year. And this is a most singular fact to one who has travelled only in Europe, that, as is the case in the United

States, trees should grow in the water, and yet not be killed. This Great Dismal was explored some years ago by Mr. Edmund Ruffin, author of the valuable Agricultural Journal. He first calls attention to the fact that a greater portion of the vast morass stands higher than the ground that surrounds it; it is a great spongy mass of peat, standing some seven or eight feet higher than its banks, as was ascertained by careful measurements when the railroad was cut through. It consists of vegetable matter, with a slight admixture of earthy substance, as in coal. The source of peat in Scotland is, that one layer of vegetation is not decomposed before another forms. So is it in Chili, Patagonia and Terra del Fuego. Thus, also, is it in different parts of Europe, in the Falkland Islands, as Darwin has shown. Thus, too, is it in the Great Dismal, where the plants and trees are different from those of the peat in New York. It is found, on cutting down the trees and draining the swamp, and letting in the sun, that the vegetation will not be supported as it was before, beneath the dark shade of the trees. In the middle is a fine lake, and the whole is inhabited by wild animals, and it is somewhat dangerous to dwell near it by reason of the bad atmosphere it creates. It is covered by most luxuriant vegetation. It is found in some places in England, that there is a species of *walking-mosses*, which are sometimes seized with a fancy to walk from their places; the moss swells up, bursts, and rolls off, sometimes burying cottages in its path. In some places this peat has been dug into and houses have been found several feet below the surface—curious antiquarian remains. In the same manner the Great Dismal may spread itself over the surrounding country.

Having thus dwelt somewhat minutely upon the coal formation, and the geological phenomena to which it is allied, we will, in conclusion, take a retrospect view of the strata of the earth, and the means which have, from time to time, modified and changed its configuration. The origin of our earth, as already intimated, must have been a mass kept in a state of fusion by heat, its surface becoming hard by being gradually cooled. The most ancient portion of the earth, therefore, is composed of granite, which appears in an unstratified mass, and bears every indication of an *igneous* origin. There are some kinds of granite, however, of comparatively recent origin, which so clearly resemble the ancient rock as to be sometimes difficult to distinguish one from the other. Gneiss is a rock very analagous to granite. It is stratified, however, and seems to have been formed under water. It alternates with mica-schist, which ordinarily accompanies granite and gneiss. Next we have argillaceous schist, which was also formed under water, and which is of a soft, slaty nature, and easily split.

These rocks, whose origin is co-eval with the creation of the earth, are frequently found at the tops of mountains, as well as at the lowest depths of valleys, which goes to prove that the earth has, at various periods, been subjected to the severest upheavals and internal convulsions. Among these rocks *no fossils* have ever been found, and it is thus certain that animal and vegetable life did not exist at this early period of the earth's history.

It is in the next, or second geological epoch, called the transition formation, that the first traces of the existence of vegetable and marine life on the surface of the globe, are found. Previous to this period, and perhaps as a prelude to the introduction of life, the former rocks had been disturbed, as above mentioned, for we do not find the strata of the transition formation in parallel layers over the primitive beds; but, on the contrary, they are deposited in the greatest apparent confusion.

Geologists have divided this formation into three divisions, which are called respectively the Cambrian, the Silurian, and the Devonian systems of rocks. The former are the oldest *sedimentary rocks* known, and are composed of schistose grauwackes, mica-schists, and gneiss. The Cambrian rocks contain organic remains of various brachipods, polyparia, coral animals, &c.

The Silurian system, which is next above the Cambrian, comprises an upper and lower stratum, and is very nearly similar to those rocks. They are exclusively of marine origin, and whole beds are composed of shells, corals, &c., and those peculiar crustacea termed *Trilobites*, and which, being rarely found in other situations, are characteristic only of the Silurian and Devonian strata.

After the revolutions which seem to have terminated the primitive epoch, the earth must have remained for a long time in a state of repose, as we find in the third geological period, denominated the secondary formation, the stratum called the *old red sandstone*, consisting of a mass of rocks and pebbles, cemented together, having been transported and accumulated through the action of water, and upon which rest the *carboniferous deposits*. This formation is composed principally of marine fossils, the varieties of which are very numerous. The mountain limestone, and metalliferous limestone, in which are found ores of lead, copper, zinc, &c., besides numerous descriptions of organic remains, belong to this formation. Next comes the *coal formation*, and, as previously stated, this is exclusively composed of vegetable matter, formed as aforesaid, and in which marine fossils are rarely found.

A violent convulsion seems to have terminated the coal period, which was succeeded by what is called the Saliferous formation— being the fourth geological epoch. In this are found the red conglomerate, new red sandstone, &c., very often deposited in layers from one to five hundred feet deep. Few organic remains are found in these beds; but it was at this time that the animals belonging to the class of reptiles were created.

In this epoch are embraced several formations, (mostly of local names,) which, not being essential to our present purpose, it is unnecessary to enumerate.

The fifth geological epoch, (in ascending order,) comprises what are called the Liassic, the Jurassic, and the Oolitic systems. Previous to this epoch, the earth was inhabited only by certain plants, and a few inferior animals and reptiles; but at the commencement of this formation, a new fauna was created, composed of animals and reptiles of strange form and gigantic size. Rocks of the Jurassic system, as also those of the Liassic, are not met with in this country, and we therefore avoid a further reference to them, as well as the fossils which they contain.

In the sixth geological epoch, also in the secondary formation, we have the lower or inferior cretaceous system, abounding, as the latter mentioned series, in marine and animal fossils. This formation contains limestone, with here and there deposits of gypsum, clays, sands, iron ores, &c. In England, under the name of *Wealden formation*, are deposited, in alternate layers, limestone, sand, and clay, all of which are frequently of great thickness. Above the Wealden formation is a group of deposits of green sand, in which are distributed particles of silicate of iron, which are also found in New Jersey. Higher up are again found limestone, sandstones, and chalk marls, the stratification of which is only indicated by layers of flint in the latter. Beds of the cretaceous group are found in New Jersey and other parts of the United States, but they rest on the oldest secondary rocks, without the intervention of the Oolite.

The next formation, (and the seventh geological epoch) is called the *Tertiary*. Between the commencement of this epoch, and the termination of the chalk strata, all traces of ancient or primitive remains are lost; the fossils which are found in the subsequent formations being but types of existing organic creatures.

The Tertiary formation is divided by geologists into the Eocene,

ANTHRACITE COAL FORMATION.

Miocene, and Pliocene; or the older, middle and newer Tertiary groups. The first named stratum is developed in the states of Virginia, North and South Carolina, Georgia, Alabama, &c. It consists principally of greenish sands, nearly identical with the cretaceous series, and of the same mineral qualities. Near Paris it embraces layers of limestones, marls, and siliceous matter;—while in London it forms stiff and again plastic clays, which are useful for manufacturing purposes. Above these layers occur various kinds of clays, limestones, marls, gypsums, &c., the latter of which are extensively used in France for the manufacture of Plaster of Paris. Above the gympsum we find a more modern group, composed of marls, sands and flints—the first a marine, and the other a fresh water deposit.

The Miocene beds prevail on the Continent of Europe, and in America along the shores of the Chesapeake Bay, and in some parts of Virginia. They abound in fossils, and consist mainly of shells, sands, sandstones, and conglomerates of gravel, which are hard enough for building stones. In some portions of the globe, the Miocene series present combustible materials—and remains of dicotyledonous plants abound in them in Switzerland, Germany and Italy.

The Pliocene beds of the United States are of comparatively recent origin. They are found in New York, Kentucky, and along the banks of the Potomac in Maryland. In Europe, *brown coal*, or lignite, is found in layers, which can be advantageously worked. The beds extend all over the old world, and their mineral properties vary in different points; at some places they exhibit evidences of far greater age than at other points. They consist mainly of marls, sands, and remains of marine, fresh water, and land animals.

In this formation are also embraced superficial deposits of drift, consisting of gravel, boulders, sand, clay, &c. There are two kinds of drift, one called the ancient or *diluvium* and the other the modern or *alluvium*. In the former, which covers over the Tertiary formation, are found fossils which date not very far back from the present period,—as the diluvial period, in a manner, unites the Tertiary with the recent past. In these deposits are found bones of extinct and recent genera of animals, and among them those of the *Magatherium*, the skeletons of which measure eighteen feet in length, and about nine feet in height. This animal is much larger than any subsequent one, and the thigh-bone is believed to be three times as great as that of any known elephant. In this formation are found remains of elephants, horses, rhinoceroses, &c., while it is to this period also that geologists refer the immense masses of debris which contain gold, platina, and the diamond, in Brazil, Africa, India, and California, as well as the veins of tin in England and Mexico. The formation known as the boulder or erratic block formation, also belongs to the diluvial period. All over the world these boulders have been deposited. In some places they are of huge proportions and weight, while ordinarily they consist of gravel stones, of more or less greatness. They are composed of various mineral material, and not unfrequently are pure and hard granite.

In the United States, many of the valleys are filled up to a great depth with the modern or alluvial deposits. They consist mostly of a heterogeneous mass of earthy matter, brought down from the higher lands by rains and freshets. Bones of the buffalo, the elephant, and other animals, are found in these beds; and skeletons of the celebrated *Mastodon* have been exhumed at different localities.

It is in the modern formation, comprising the eighth geological epoch, that the first traces of the human family have been discovered; and although it is possible that its origin may date farther back than can be supposed from the evidences furnished by the exposed land, yet geologists generally unite in the belief that no earlier records appear in that portion of the earth covered by the sea.

Immediately previous to the modern epoch the earth seems to have enjoyed a repose of long duration. With the exception of a few upheavals occurring during the latter portion of the diluvial period, there has been no catastrophe of any moment; and all the changes which have taken place "since the great flood" have been brought about by various causes—by those gradual and almost imperceptible agencies which, continuing from century to century, and from thousandth year to thousandth year, will sooner or later have brought the world to another grand epoch.

Having thus desultorily traced the order of strata, we may add that it is always *regular*. We can never find coal, for example, below the more *ancient* formations; though we often see ancient rocks overlaying modern formations, the result of recent eruptions and upheavals. Thus we perceive the value, in an economical view, of scientific knowledge. Thousands of dollars have been, and are still expended by the uninformed, in explorations after mineral treasure, which, did they but enjoy a limited knowledge of those paramount

ANTHRACITE COAL FORMATION. 143

laws which pervade throughout all the Creator's works, could be saved; besides the labor, anxiety, and bitter disappointments which invariably attend ill-directed enterprises.

In casting our eye over the surface of the earth, we everywhere perceive evidences of a universal and continual change. The frosts of autumn, the snows of winter, the rains of spring, the electricity of the summer—each contribute to this purpose. The substance of mountains is daily diminishing; and rocks, those silent historians of the past, gradually crumble into atoms, and unperceived, are borne off to new resting-places in the deep green ocean. Here they enter into new combinations, and by earthquakes and volcanic action, as well as by the natural accumulation of the beds, again appear to the

FIG. 19.

light of day, throwing back the surrounding waters, and presenting new "isles in the watery waste." Finally, one little island effects a friendly union with another, and thus, age after age, century after century, the undeviating, the everlasting laws of the great God are performing the functions contemplated in the creation.

Although our limits will not allow a minute description of the varied strata of the earth's crust, yet it is necessary to a proper elucidation of what has already been said as well as what is to follow, to point out some of the changes of position, of fracture, denudation and disruption which they have undergone. Fig. 18, will probably serve to show the original horizontal appearance of strata, one layer lying upon another. Fig. 19 exhibits the usual appearance of stratified rocks, lying also in a horizontal position, the lines of stratification being distinctly marked, dividing the rocks into layers very nearly

FIG. 20.

detached from each other. This is peculiar to all aqueous rocks, and may be noticed in quarries of limestone, and similar stratified rocks. From a horizontal position, owing to the disturbing causes previously enumerated, the strata have in many instances been changed to a vertical position, as shown in fig. 20.

In other cases, they are changed to an inverted position by the intrusion of igneous rocks from below, and actually thrown back, as

FIG. 21.

exhibited in fig. 21. Sometimes the strata are disjointed, and fig. 22 represents a similar instance to the above of change in the direction, probably produced by a like cause; for the beds which at b, strike in a southerly direction, on reaching a, are thrown into vertical and dis-

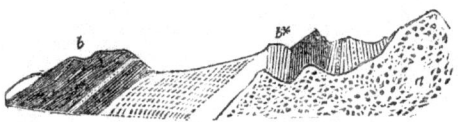

FIG. 22.

jointed masses at b^*. In other instances, the strata are *curved*, as is frequently the case with gneiss, especially in the Isle of Wight, a delineation of an instance of which forms the frontispiece of Dr. McCullough's Western Isles, from which fig. 23 is extracted. In many cases, especially in the anthracite coal districts, the strata have a waving or arched position, similar to that indicated in fig. 23, while in other cases they are frightfully contorted, as illustrated in fig. 24.

ANTHRACITE COAL FORMATION.

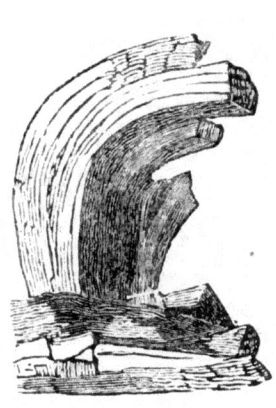

FIG. 23.   FIG. 24.

Such contortions were shown by Sir James Hall, by a simple experiment, to have resulted from lateral pressure, attended with some degree of resistance, both above and beneath. He took several pieces of cloth—some cotton, some linen—and having placed them horizontally on a table, *c*, fig. 25, covered them by a weight, *a*, placed also horizontally on the pieces of cloth. He then exposed

FIG. 25.   FIG. 26.

the *sides to pressure*, upon which the curved appearance indicated in fig. 26 was the result. It is thus that, by the chemical operations within the interior of the earth, the strata have been contorted and thrown into every imaginable shape and position, while the unstratified rocks have, at the same time, been heaved up, and thrown around in irregular shapes and quantities. The **unstratified**, which are the oldest of all rocks, differ from the sedimentary principally in having no lines or parallel markings; but present a shapeless and irregular mass of mineral matter, similar to fig. 27. But

FIG. 27.

while the granite, and other rocks of igneous origin, are unstratified, they still occur in veins, which are sometimes traversed by other veins newer than themselves. This is illustrated in fig. 28, where the new veins project over the old granite somewhat like the horns of a deer. These veins often penetrate the overlying deposits, and flow over the rocks which they displace, as exhibited in fig. 29.

FIG. 28.   FIG. 29.

Sometimes they are so small that the markings of the cleavage are scarcely visible, yet they still resemble stratification, and might readily be mistaken for such. This deceptive appearance is often

ANTHRACITE COAL FORMATION.

presented at the junction of granite with slate, and may readily be detected by observing the distinct mineral character of the two rocks. Some of the unstratified rocks, more especially basalt and greenstone, occasionally assume a columnar form, as indicated in fig. 30.

FIG. 30.

These columns are of various sizes, but have most generally from four to six sides. They vary, however, in length and shape, not unfrequently appearing in short blocks or prisms—sometimes standing vertically or inclined, and at others laying horizontally. In the celebrated Giant's Causeway, where they occur in a tabular mass, the columns are nearly in a vertical position, as illustrated in the engraving.

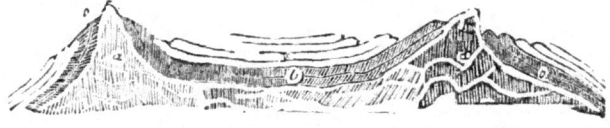

FIG. 31.

We have thus briefly described the unstratified rocks as constituting the frame-work or foundation of the whole superstructure of the globe. The accompanying figure, 31, exhibits the varied situations of the granite, (the oldest rock of the earth,) as forming the foundation upon which all the others repose, and the nucleus of the mountain, which, having been forced through the superincumbent rocks, has borne them upwards in its ascent; the strata in the vicinity of the mountain, *a*, being raised at an acute angle at *b*, and sinking to nearly a level position in the plains at *c*. The form and succession of these rocks, says Prof. Richardson, prevail all over the earth, with some local exceptions; so that its entire surface may be considered to form a series of basins, of which the largest, deepest, and thickest lie at the bottom, and are filled up by others, which become smaller, shallower and thinner as they approach the top—the deposits being uplifted and raised towards the edges of these basins, and become level, or nearly so, towards the centre.

The inclination of strata from a horizontal position is called their dip, the amount of the dip being the quantity of the angle which the line of inclination makes with that of the horizon, as in the accompanying figure, 32. If the angle made by the meeting of the lines

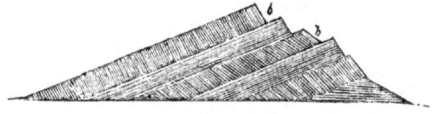

FIG. 32.

of the strata, *bb*, and the horizontal line, *a*, be equal to forty-five degrees towards the east, the strata are said to dip to that extent in that direction. Again, the terms *dip* and *strike* of strata will be further understood—(for these are terms in universal use in mining,) by the following illustration: The dip, as before observed, is the line which the strata makes with the horizon—the *strike* being a line at right angles to the dip. To illustrate; place a book on a table, with the edges of the leaves downwards, and the back of the book upwards, as in the accompanying figure, 33. If one side of the cover be removed a short distance, the cover so moved, *b*, will represent the line of *dip*, while the back of the volume, *a, a*, will exemplify the line of *strike*. If the cover of the book be extended only in a slight degree, the dip, of course, will be proportionally steep, and *vice versa*. Having thus ascertained the line of dip, we can determine the probable direction of the strike—for if the dip be towards the north or south, the strike will be east and west; and *vice versa*.

FIG. 33.

ANTHRACITE COAL FORMATION.

But the converse of this proposition by no means holds good; for though the line of dip gives the line of strike, the line of strike does not give the line of dip, since there are *two* lines of dip common to every line of strike; and strata having a line of strike running from north to south, may *dip* either to the east or west. In short, as we have moved one side of the cover of our book to the right, we can move the other to the left *b*, (fig. 34,) while the *back* of the volume, *a, a*, remains in the same position. The terms anticlinal and synclinal lines are frequently used in mining phraseology. The anticlinal line is, simply, that elevated central point from which the strata *diverge* in opposite directions. To illustrate this, we have only to extend both sides of our volume, as in fig. 35. The synclinal line is exactly the *reverse* of the above, being the point at which the strata *converge* towards each other. To illustrate this, we have merely to turn our book over, and open it only half-way, exactly in the middle, and the line between the two pages will present the synclinal line, or that point *towards* which the strata tend, as exhibited in fig. 36.

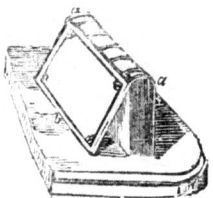

FIG. 34.

FIG. 35.

FIG. 36.

In speaking of strata, in mining phraseology, they are said to be *conformable* when their general planes are parallel, no matter what may be their dip, as in figure 37, where both the upper horizontal strata, *a*, and the lower inclined series *b*, are conformable to each other. When a series of upper strata, however, rest on a lower formation, without any conformity to the position of the latter, they bespeak a more modern series, showing that the *newest* of the underlaying group must have been deposited before the oldest of the latter. They thus occupy an unconformable position, as exhibited in the same fig. 37, wherein the upper horizontal beds, *a*, are unconformable to the lower inclined deposits, *b*. This simple illustration is very important, because it often shows the position of coal veins

FIG. 37.

lying in an unconformable position to the more modern overlaying surface.

Various writers have cautioned the observer against certain deceptive appearances of the strata in particular lines of coast, (which are no less frequent in our mountain regions,) where beds, apparently horizontal, in reality dip at a very considerable angle. The following fig. 38, exhibits a headland as seen from the south, in which the strata appear to the eye perfectly level. There appears to be no mistake about their horizontal position; but if the headland treads

FIG. 38.

off, at the point p, in fig. 39, to the northward, affording a view of the cliffs westward, it will be seen that the appearance from the south is defective, for the lines here show a considerable angle to the north, and gradually increasing in their dip, finally become *vertical* at a.

It has already been intimated that fossiliferous rocks follow an invariable *order* of succession, but that the arrangement, although never reversed, is sometimes imperfect; so that, while we never meet b going before a, or c preceding b, yet we occasionally miss not only a single letter, but a succession of letters, and find, in certain locali-

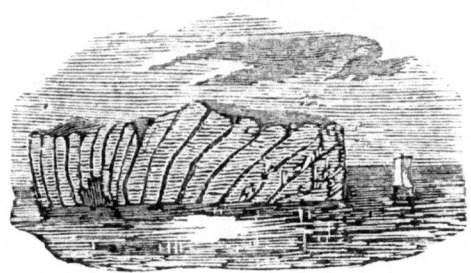

FIG. 39.

ties, that entire groups of strata are wanting, which occur in other places of like geological character. This effect may have resulted either from the missing beds never having been deposited in this spot, or from their having been denuded, and carried away by the abrading power of water, before the new strata were deposited. Similar causes may have occasioned either the partial deposition, or partial denudation of a single bed, and produced the thinning out of a particular stratum, as exhibited in fig. 40. The conformable or unconformable position of the strata affords a safe and satisfactory guide to many investigations of interest and great practical importance. From data thus furnished, we learn that the mountain-chains were not all of contemporaneous origin, but have been raised at different periods, and sometimes under different circumstances and agencies. Thus, if on the sides of one mountain, fig. 41, we find a series of strata, a, raised and covered unconformably by another group, b, it is obvious that the central chain must have been thrown up *after* the series a had been deposited, but *before* the formation of the beds b. But if, on the sides of another mountain, fig. 42, we find both the series a and b tilted, and covered unconformably by another series c, we have proofs *that this mountain chain* is of more modern date than that on the sides of which the same strata, b, are undisturbed.

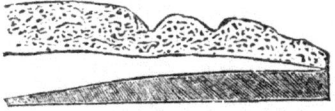

FIG. 40.

We have already remarked, that in all mineral regions, and espe-

FIG. 41.

cially in that of coal, where the basins are generally more or less disturbed—as, from the very nature of the deposit, they must be—the dip and strike of the strata are matters of great practical moment. Prof. Richardson, in his geological work, supposes a case, where a land-owner, aware that coal exists on an adjacent estate, is desirous

FIG. 42.

of ascertaining whether it may also be found on his own, and whether an attempt to discover it might be instituted with probabilities of success. In this case, the dip is almost the sole reliance. If the dip of the strata in the vicinity be *towards* the land where the trial is to be made, it is highly probable that the coal may be found under

FIG. 43.

it; but if it is in a contrary direction, the search ought not to be undertaken (unless, on examination, the veins should prove to be broken, and have a backward pitch.) The lines outcroping at the surface, fig. 43, and numbered 1, 2, 3 and 4, represent coal veins, dipping towards d, on the right-hand side; the unconformable strata, $c\ c$, are beds of sandstone lying over the coal veins. Supposing coal

ANTHRACITE COAL FORMATION. 153

vein No. 4 to rise to the surface at that point on the estate of A, adjoining the estate of B, which lies towards d: it is apparent that A would find only a point of the vein on his land, and that it would be useless to search in the direction of b for it, since the dip of the veins is sufficient to show that none exists there. But on the estate of B, though no coal came to the surface, still the dip of that which exists on the estate of A, would render it probable that coal could be readily found—the circumstances of its lying too deep for successful mining being considerations which would depend very much on the angle of dip, and the nature of its position in other respects. Strata are said to form outlayers when they constitute an isolated portion, detached from the principal mass of the same bed or region of which they once

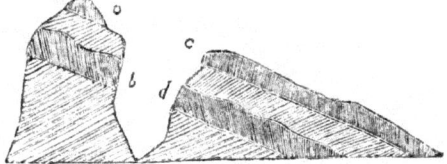

FIG. 44.

formed a part. (The anthracite coal regions are merely outlayers of the great Alleghany bituminous field, which originally comprised one immense body.) Thus, in fig. 44, the beds a and b form outlayers of the main strata, c and d—the *missing* portion having been removed by denundation, while their original identity is fully established by the accordance of the mineral deposit and position. Strata are also said to form an escarpement when terminating abruptly, as in the above figure, a and b.

The origin of valleys has most generally been referred to the agency of water; but there are other causes besides this. The surface, as

FIGURE 45.

well as the interior strata, are first dislocated by enormous fissures, caused by the upheaval of the region of which they form a part.

Fig. 45 represents such an upheaval, and shows the steep **escarpements** which follow as a natural consequence. It is in these fissures, therefore, that the formation of valleys commences, gradually enlarging until two or more unite. It is thus that most of the mountains east of the Alleghany have been formed, the water traversing them having carried off the material lying over them, and thus left steep and

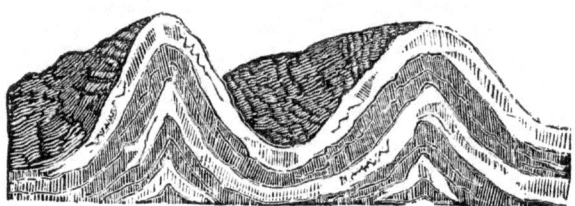

FIGURE 46.

rugged ridges, with narrow intervening valleys. Valleys of undulation, however, are produced directly by two neighboring elevations,

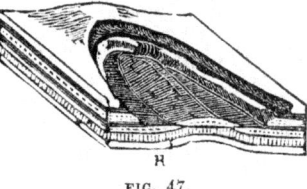

FIG. 47.

which, by lifting the strata on either side without occasioning fracture, leave the valley between. This is the most usual structure of the coal beds of Schuylkill County, fig. 46, and hence it follows that that county contains a much greater amount of mineral, in proportion to the superficial area, than any other district in the United States. The whole county is but a succession of wave-like elevations, with narrow intervening valleys, all of which are full of the valuable mineral for which the region is so remarkable. Valleys of erosion are formed by the action of water. Imagine a nearly level plain, and then, at one end of it let a stream of water issue forth: in a comparatively short time, with the assistance of snows and rains, and alternate dry seasons, it will scoop out a hollow similar to fig. 47, while, in course of time, it will form a deep valley, surrounded with high elevations, or table-lands. The Alleghanies have, for the most part, been scooped out in this manner, and the debris deposited in the table-flats sloping out from its loftier ranges.

ANTHRACITE COAL FORMATION.

The word *fault* is one very extensively used in mining, and refers to the dislocations which interrupt the continuity of the strata. They are of various kinds and forms, and constitute a source of great expense and annoyance in mining coal. Fig. 48 represents an example, where the strata, which were once continuous, either by their subsidence on one side, or their elevation on the other, have been dislocated and displaced.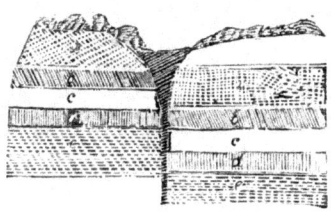

FIG. 48.

Suppose that b, on the left, were a coal vein: on arriving at the *fault*, and penetrating it, the coal vein is lost, and a great expense necessarily ensues before it can be found. While faults are a source of great annoyance, generally speaking, they still afford some corresponding advantages, since they somewhat counteract the tendency of the coal veins—pitching, as they do in this region, at a steep angle, to plunge into inaccessible depths; and when the fissures are filled with solid rocks, as they most generally are, they form strong supports for the overlaying strata, as well as embankments to keep back the water from the mine. There is, we have stated, a

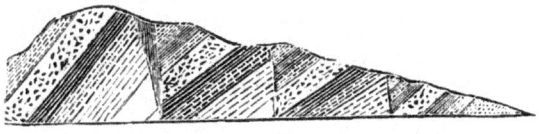

FIG. 49.

variety of faults, both of rock and clay, or soft earth. We present another idea in reference to them, in fig. 49, where the strata have been still more disturbed than in the preceding.

We have thus, somewhat briefly, pointed out some of the leading features constituting the vegetation and stratification of the coal formation; to dwell upon them at greater length than is necessary to sustain the tenor of our object, would be a waste of time, and would usurp too much of our space. For much of what has been said, we are indebted to the able geological works of Prof. Richardson, and acknowledge our obligations with a high sense of appreciation of his researches. With these examples, therefore, we must leave this branch of the subject, and proceed to the direct consideration of the great anthracite coal beds now before us.

DISCOVERY OF ANTHRACITE COAL.

The discovery of coal in the Lehigh district is said to have been purely accidental. There had been legends of long standing, supposed to have emanated from the Indians, that coal abounded in this section of Pennsylvania; and among some of the credulous German farmers in Lehigh, Berks, Lancaster, &c., one is occasionally reminded of them, and grave intimations thrown out that coal is reposing in "certain places" beneath the luxuriant soil of those counties. Such traditionary reports prevailed for a long time among the early settlers of the territory now comprising the several counties of the anthracite regions, and if similar ones in the counties above named should ever be realized in the same happy manner, all will unite in admiration of the German stoicism with which they are still maintained by the "older inhabitants." The story of its discovery near Mauch Chunk, in the present county of Carbon, is doubtless already familiar to many. Nevertheless, it is so curious and romantic in itself, and is fraught with such miraculous results upon the physical and mental condition of mankind, that we cannot omit it here. The account was given by the late Dr. James, of Philadelphia, who, in the year 1804, in company with Anthony Morris, Esq. of the same city, visited some lands, held jointly by them, near Sharp Mountain.

"In the course of our pilgrimage, we reached the summit of Mauch Chunk mountain, the present site of anthracite coal. At the time there were only to be seen three or four small pits, which had the appearance of the commencement of rude wells, into one of which our guide, Philip Ginter, descended with great ease, and threw up some pieces of coal for our examination. After which, whilst we lingered on the spot, contemplating the wildness of the scene, honest Philip amused us with the following narrative of the original discovery of this most valuable of minerals, now promising, from its general diffusion, so much of wealth and comfort to a great portion of the United States.

"He said that when he first took up his residence in that district of country, he built himself a rough cabin in the forest, and supported his family by the proceeds of his rifle; being literally a hunter of the backwoods. The game he shot, including bear and deer, he carried to the nearest store, and exchanged for other necessaries of life. But at this particular time, to which he then alluded, he was without a supply of food for his family; and after being out all day with his gun in quest of it, he was returning, towards evening, over the Mauch Chunk mountain, entirely unsuccessful and disappointed; a drizzling rain beginning to fall, and night rapidly approaching, he bent his course homeward, considering himself one of the most *forsaken* of human beings. As he strode slowly over the ground, his foot stumbled against something, which, by the stroke, was driven before him; observing it to be black, to distinguish which there was just light enough remaining, he took it up, and as he had often listened to the traditions of the country of the existence of coal in the vicinity, it occurred to him that this might be a portion of that *stonecoal*, of which he had heard. He accordingly carefully took it with him to the cabin, and the next day carried it to Colonel Jacob Weiss, residing at what was then known by the name of Fort Allen— (erected under the auspices of Dr. Franklin.) The Colonel, who was alive to the subject, brought the specimen with him to Philadelphia, and submitted it to the inspection of John Nicholson and Michael Hillegas, Esqs., and also to Charles Cist, a printer, who ascertained its nature and qualities, and authorized the Colonel to pay Ginter for his discovery, upon his pointing out the precise spot where he found the coal. This was readily done by acceding to Ginter's proposal of getting, through the regular forms of the patent-office, the title for a small tract of land, which he supposed had never been taken up, comprising the mill-seat on which he afterwards built the mill which afforded us the lodging of the preceding night, and which he afterwards was unhappily deprived of by the claim of a prior survey."

Coal was known to exist in the vicinity of Pottsville more than seventy years ago, and searches for it had been made repeatedly—but the coal found was so different from any previously known, that it was deemed utterly valueless—more especially as no means could be devised to burn it. Searches for it were abandoned, at least for a time, when a blacksmith, by the name of Whetstone, luckily chanced upon some, and immediately undertook to use it in his shop. After experimenting with it for a short time, his efforts proved successful, and his triumph having been duly communicated, in the shape of local gossip, to the citizens of the surrounding neighborhood, attention was very soon after directed to the expediency of instituting further inquiries as to the nature and extent of the deposit, and its applicability for other purposes. Among those who at a very early period did not hesitate to declare his belief in the existence of coal in this district, was the late Judge Cooper; and it was through the influence of such persons that searches were continued through circumstances and prejudices at once discouraging, and seemingly foolhardy. Among the first, if they were not the first, who undertook explorations for coal, were the Messrs. Potts. They made examinations at various points along the old Sunbury road, but in no instance did success attend them. The late William Morris, soon after the operations of Messrs. Potts were terminated, became proprietor of most of the lands lying at the head of the Schuylkill; and about the year 1800 he was fortunate enough to find coal, and in the same year took a considerable quantity to Philadelphia. It was in vain that he held forth its peculiar virtues, and vast future importance—all his efforts to convince the people of its adaptation to use proved abortive; and when, occasionally, an individual was found who could be induced, through the force of argument and eloquence, to coincide in the merits of "stone-coal," the well-known lines—

> A man convinced against his *will*,
> Is of the same opinion still—

would be involuntarily forced upon his mind; and finally he had no other alternative but to dispose of his lands, and abandon his projects as altogether fruitless.

We do not know that any farther notice had now been taken of this coal, for six or seven years afterwards. Peter Bastons made some discoveries of its deposit, while erecting the Forge in Schuylkill Valley; and a blacksmith, named David Berlin, continued to improve upon the suggestions of Whetstone, (who, by this time, had discontinued business, and perhaps left the vicinity) and imparted his successes freely to others of his craft. But few, however, could be prevailed upon to use it. Prejudice—prejudice was ever keen, and it seemed to keep men of ordinary spirit at a respectful distance. Men of iron nerve could only oppose themselves to the current.

In the latter part of the year 1810, a practical chemist, combining science with practice, made such an analysis of the coal of this region, as convinced him that there was inherent in the mass all the properties suitable for combustion. He therefore erected a furnace in a small vacant house on Front street, between Philadelphia and Kensington, to which he applied three strong bellows. By this means he obtained such an immense *white heat* from the coal, that platina itself could have been melted! From this experiment was derived such proofs of its qualities, as ultimately favored its general introduction into that city.

But although it might easily be inferred that such experiments could not fail to have secured for it immediate favor, yet such was by no means the fact. Intelligent men, it is true, calmly deliberated over the subject, but that was all—the time had not yet come to act. Two years after this, the late Col. George Shoemaker and Nicholas Allen discovered coal on a piece of land which they had but recently purchased—in times past called Centreville—situate about one mile from Pottsville. They raised several wagon-loads of it, but no purchaser could be found. Mr. Allen soon became disheartened, and disposed of his interest in the lands to his partner; who, having received some encouragement from certain citizens of Philadelphia, persevered in his operations. He got out a considerable quantity, and forwarded ten wagon-loads to Philadelphia, in quest of a market. Its arrival there was, as usual, greeted with the warmest *prejudice*, and there were few who appeared to evince any curiosity or interest in the subject. Nearly every one considered it a sort of *stone*, and, saving that it was a "peculiar stone"—a stone-coal—they would as soon have thought of making fire with any other kind of *stone!* Among all those who examined the coals, but few persons could be prevailed upon to purchase, and they only a small quantity, "to try it;" but alas! the trials were unsuccessful! The purchasers denounced Colonel Shoemaker as a vile imposter and an arrant cheat! Their denunciations went forth throughout the city, and Col. Shoemaker, to escape an arrest for swindling and imposture, with which he was threatened, drove thirty miles out of his way, in *a circuitous route, to avoid the officers of the law!* He returned home, heart-sick with his adventure. But, fortunately, among the few purchasers of his coal, were a firm of iron factors in Delaware county, who, having used it successfully, proclaimed the astounding fact in the newspapers of the day. The current of prejudice thereafter began to waver somewhat; and new experiments were made at iron works on the Schuylkill, with like success, the result of which was also announced by the press. From this time, anthracite began gradually to put down its enemies—and among the more intelligent people, its future value was predicted.

The first successful experiment to *generate steam* with anthracite coal, was made in 1825, at the iron works at Phœnixville. Previously, however, John Price Wetherill, of Philadelphia, made several efforts to accomplish this, at his lead works—but we have understood that he only partially succeeded.

We will now pass by three or four years, during which little worthy of note occurred, and behold the coal trade, in the first smiles of infancy, starting into active existence. As early as 1812 the forests in the neighborhood of Philadelphia, and the vicinity of many of the principal towns of the adjoining counties, began rapidly to disappear. Cord wood, and every description of building timber, were held at high prices—the former, during the winter months, frequently ranging between thirteen and sixteen dollars per cord. There were no improvements except turnpike roads, by which the magnificent timber of some of the more distant counties could be reached; and under these circumstances, and as population and business increased, attention was directed to the necessity of rendering navigable the Schuylkill river. It was originally designed for the products of the forest, the mine, and the field; all of which abounded in the counties drained by this stream, and its numerous tributaries. The forests, especially, were remarkable for the quality of the timber, and the height and symmetrical beauty of the trees; and among intelligent capitalists little doubt was now entertained as to the destiny which awaited the product of the mine—satisfied that it needed but a fair start to ensure its onward progress.

We have thus glanced at some of the leading incidents connected with the early history of the coal trade; it now remains to consider the position, dimensions, and structure of the coal basins themselves, which, ever since their discovery, have annually grown in value and importance, and, in their future bearing upon the economy of trade, are more important to the people of Pennsylvania than all the gold of California.

ANTHRACITE COAL FORMATION.

GEOGRAPHICAL POSITION OF THE COAL REGIONS.

LOCALITY.—The anthracite formation of Pennsylvania lies in the Counties of Schuylkill, Dauphin, Lebanon, Carbon, Northumberland, Columbia, and Luzerne, in the middle part of the Eastern portion of the State. It is watered by the Susquehanna, Schuylkill, and Lehigh rivers, and their numerous tributary branches.

EXTENT.—The anthracite formation of Pennsylvania may be divided into three grand divisions, or large coal regions; the first, or most southern division, being known as the South Anthracite Region; the second division called the Middle Anthracite Region, and the third grand division is known as the North Anthracite Region, or Wyoming Coal-field.

The three great anthracite regions may again be divided into coal districts, as follows, viz.: The coal districts contained in the south anthracite region, commencing at its eastern end, and continuing thence westward, are the Lehigh, Tamaqua, Tuscarora, Schuylkill Valley, Pottsville, Minersville, Swatara, and the Lykens' Valley, and Dauphin—the Lykens' Valley being the north fork, and the Dauphin the south fork of the western extension of the south anthracite region.

The middle anthracite region, commencing at the western end, and continuing thence eastward, has the Shamokin, Mahanoy, Girardsville, and Quaquake coal districts; together with the small detached coal basins contiguous to the Lehigh river, as the Beaver Meadow, Hazleton, Black Creek, Sandy Creek, and others of still smaller area.

The north anthracite region, commencing west and continuing thence north-eastward, has the Shickshinny, Wilkesbarre, Newport, Pittston, Lackawanna, and Carbondale coal districts.

The south anthracite region extends in length from its eastern point-like end, near the Lehigh, to its western terminus near the Susquehanna—a distance of about seventy-five miles. The greatest breadth, including the coal formation on Broad Mountain, is about six miles. This measurement is across the widest and central portion of the region, and will only hold good for a short distance. The average width of coal ground of the south anthracite region is not more than about two miles. This region, as has already been remarked, is spread

14 *   V

like a canoe, being broadest at Pottsville, and gradually contracting at each end at the Susquehanna and the Lehigh. Thus, at Tamaqua, sixteen miles east of Pottsville, the basin is a little more than a mile in width, and the arrangement of the strata is exhibited in the following figure, 50, which we extract from the book of the late Richard C. Taylor.

The middle anthracite region, with the detatched coal basins at its eastern part, on the Lehigh, extends in length to its point-like terminus at its western end, which point is about seven miles east from the river Susquehanna—a distance of about fifty miles. The middle region will average nearly as much *coal ground* as the first named region.

The north anthracite region extends from its north-eastern end, on the head waters of Lackawanna creek, to its western point at Skickshinny, on the north branch of the Susquehanna, a distance of upwards of sixty miles. This will not average so great an area of coal ground as either of the other two great regions.

Within the limits of the three great anthracite regions, are ridges and spaces composed of conglomerate, red shale, and sandstone strata, which lie between, and separate from each other the several basins of each of the three great divisions. In this stratification no coal exists. The value of the land which contains the coal is calculated by taking into consideration the number, thickness, character, and quality of the veins of mineral in each particular place, and from their adaptation for mining to advantage, and their accessibility to market.

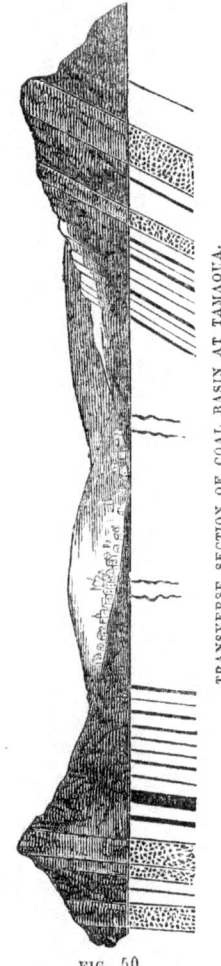

FIG. 50.

TRANSVERSE SECTION OF COAL BASIN AT TAMAQUA.

GEOLOGICAL CHARACTER OF THE ANTHRACITE COAL FORMATION.

The anthracite formation of Pennsylvania, as regards its geological character, especially in the south region, is very much distorted, and the coal veins disturbed, and irregular in their courses. In working the mines *faults*, both of a hard and soft nature, or, in other words, rock and slate, (or what is not inappropriately named *dirt faults*, some of which are of great magnitude) are frequently met with, which not only prove a great loss to the owners of the properties in which they occur, by diminishing the quantity of coal, but are often a serious inconvenience to the prosecution of the mine, and a great drawback upon the profits of the operators and lessees of the colliery, sometimes occasioning the abandonment of the work altogether.

In the middle anthracite region, taking as an index the mines in operation, the explorations already made, and the general kind appearance of the rocks, and great regularity of the surface, it is presumed that faults will not be found to exist to any great extent. Indeed, the whole geological character of the middle anthracite region—the general order and range of the stratification being so uniform and undisturbed—goes far to prove that *faults* of any magnitude will be rarely encountered. The mountains are very high, the coal veins, especially those of the bottom part of the series, are generally thick, and crop out high up the mountain sides; therefore, an inexhaustable amount of coal, of the very best quality, may be safely calculated upon as existing in this coal region.

In the north region the general character of the strata is undulating, and comparatively flat to what is found in the south or middle regions. The coal veins, which are those of the bottom of the formation, are generally of great thickness, and of good quality, but in quantity there is not that average amount per acre of coal as is found in the other great regions. This may be accounted for from the slightly undulating arrangement of the strata, and from the waters of the North Branch of the Susquehanna River, which flow through the central part of the coal valley, having changed its course from time to time, and swept or washed away much of the coal, leaving in places sand and gravel banks that cover considerable area of surface. The great Wyoming flats indicate the change which has taken place in the course of the river.

The basis of the anthracite formation of Pennsylvania is a conglomerate rock, consisting of white quartz pebbles of various sizes, imbedded in a strong siliceous cement; underneath the conglomerate is a thick mass of red shale and sandstone strata, which completely encircles, in a continuous mountain chain, the three great anthracite regions of the State.

The conglomerate, where the measures are perpendicular, forms high massive walls of rock on the summit of the mountains which bound the coal regions, and divide the coal basins; and it is of such a durable, undecomposing nature, that in some places where the strata is on edge, it rises a natural wall twenty to thirty feet in height above the level of the crest of the mountain, and not more than from two to three feet in thickness from the base up. In other places it lies *en masse* in immense blocks, covered with a variety of moss—giving it an imposing, extraordinary rough, and romantic appearance, as in the valley of the Swatara, Wolf Creek, etc.

As the coal measures—from their highly inclined angle of dip, which are in some places in the mountain that forms the southern boundary of the south anthracite coal region, overtilted—pass to a lesser angle of inclination, which gradually decreases in proceeding northward over the three great anthracite regions—the conglomerate becomes more thin and less abrupt in its character; and, indeed, its situation is at times only marked by the loose detached white pebble stones scattered over the surface of the ground, the cement which binds the parts together being in some situations of a more decomposing quality than it is at other places.

The red shale, by exposure to the air, and by the action of water, decomposes very freely, and is the great reason why the general character of the mountains which form the boundaries of the coal regions are so steep as they are found to be where streams of any size run along their base; while the conglomerate on their summits remains undisturbed a rock of ages, until the red shale, on which it reposes, crumbles away, and thus these immense rocks are hurled from their elevated natural position into the valleys below, and thus are immense boulders of the conglomerate carried away from their native beds to great distances.

The south anthracite region contains several elongated synclinal and anticlinal axis of stratification. The general order of the coal veins range parallel with the mountain chains that bound the sides

ANTHRACITE COAL FORMATION.   165

of the troughs or basins, which is in an east and west direction—the general *dip* of the veins being north and south.

The first or south axis or trough of coal strata, of the south anthracite region, is bounded by Sharp Mountain on the south, and by a range of hills, parallel with Sharp Mountain, on the north. This axis is in shape like a *canoe*, its greatest width being about the town of Pottsville, which, in that place, is something over half a mile. The eastern terminus of this axis is a short distance south-east of Middleport. The western terminus is near the Susquehanna. Its continuation westward forms the southern fork of coal strata in Dauphin district. The extreme length of this axis is about fifty miles. At each terminus of this axis or trough of coal strata, the bottom veins end in a point, and are considerably elevated above the place of the same veins in the central part.

In the commencement of mining operations in Schuylkill county, and indeed down to the present time, it has been considered by many persons who profess a knowledge of these matters, that the range of Coal veins in Sharp Mountain, which are what is termed *overtilted* from the perpendicular, are not identical with those veins worked on the opposite side of this narrow trough or synclinal axis—*i. e.* they are not the uprising to the south of the coal veins worked in the range of hills on the north side of the trough, and which dip to the south, and the sections hitherto made and published tend to show that the veins on the north side of the axis are not connected with those of Sharp Mountain. It is true that the coal veins of both sides of this synclinal axis dip in the same direction to the south—those of Sharp Mountain on the south side the axis at an angle of about 80° to 85°, and those on the hills on the north side the axis, at an angle of 45° to 50°, and 60°,—yet there is ample evidence to prove the fact that the south and north ranges *connect with each other*, and will be found to basin beneath the surface in the valley.

In an excavation at Pottsville, made in the centre of the two ranges of coal strata of the first or south synclinal axis, is developed the curvature of the axis,—the stratification of rock overlaying the upper vein of coal is regularly continued and unbroken from one side of the range to the other, and at the extreme ends of this elongated trough, from the bottom veins of coal being highly elevated, and their dip thereby considerably decreased, they show the axis to be perfect throughout, and the south and north ranges identical and connected with each other. Thus we have at the extreme ends of the first synclinal axis, the bottom, and in the centre of it, the top of the stratification of which it is composed, in a perfect and regular basin-like and synclinal order—clearly connecting the coal veins which are found in Sharp Mountain, the south side of the axis, with those in the small range of hills, the north side of the axis.

A very important experiment has recently been made at St. Clair, in this basin, which goes to prove that the white ash veins of Mine Hill and Broad Mountain run into the Schuylkill basin, where they underlie the red ash coal. At the anticlinal axis, at the place above named, a shaft was lately sunk, which, after penetrating about a hundred and fifty yards, struck a vein of white ash coal, lying nearly horizontal, and thirty feet in thickness. The result of this discovery is, that the Schuylkill basin necessarily contains a much larger amount of coal, to the acre, than any other basin of either of the three great regions, and from its position at the head of navigation, renders the value of the land correspondingly great. The value of coal land, in this basin, is moreover greatly increased by the inclined position which the coal strata occupy, thus affording a greater *amount of coal to the acre*, than if they lay flat or horizontal. An acre of coal land, in Schuylkill county, estimated at twenty-five cents per ton, is worth from twenty to thirty thousand dollars, and it will not be long before such prices, high as they may now seem, will be freely realized. A single vein of coal in the Mine Hill region, for several years past, has returned an annual rental of over $62,000 to the proprietors, from four or five colliery works in operation upon it; and the same tract will probably continue to yield a like sum for many years to come.

A prejudice against the productive value of coal lands was early created by the scenes of speculation which formerly involved them, and from their outside connection with ill-conceived improvements. The day for speculation, however, is about disappearing; and people are now awaking to a sense of the true and *bona fide* value of coal lands, which must henceforth greatly increase with the increasing annual demands of the trade. We repeat, therefore, what we know to be the fact, that an acre of coal land, favorably situated in Schuylkill county is worth, on a fair average, at least three times the amount of money of a similar acre, situated in other districts where the strata are horizontal, the veins *flatened out*, the coal necessarily soft, and the facilities for mining correspondingly impaired. The value of Schuylkill county land is also greatly increased by the facilities for transportation to market, the numerous lateral roads penetrating every coal district, and the *natural adaptation* of the county for mining purposes. In respect to market, this coal region is the nearest, and for all time to come must rule the destiny of the trade. The real future value of its coal land is, in our opinion, far beyond estimate. The gold of California, centred in one huge stupendous lump, could not purchase a single basin of it, were we the fortunate owner!

In his description of the Sharp Mountain range of coal strata, our State Geologist and myself* do not agree, and it may not be out of place here to give his remarks thereon in full, with the reason why my opinion and his are at variance with each other, as to this particular part of the coal formation. Prof. Rogers, in his second report on the Geological exploration of Pennsylvania, p. 80, says: "By far the most conspicuous north and south disruption of the coal measures and their southern conglomerate barrier, is displayed in an enormous dislocation of the entire chain of the Sharp Mountain, about nine miles east of Pottsville, by which the whole mass of the mountain on the eastern side of the break, has been moved northward, through at least one-fourth of a mile, throwing, of course, all the coal seams far out of their regular position." From a careful examination of the place referred to by Professor Rogers, as above, I find that no evidence is shown that the coal measures of Sharp Mountain have been moved northward, or in any way displaced; but, on the contrary, a uniform regularity is maintained in this part of the coal region. The Sharp Mountain, it is true, is not continued eastward further than the place referred to, for the reason that the coal measures of the first synclinal axis of the south anthracite region having terminated there. The coal veins of this axis, as I before observed, are gradually elevated as they approach this point, one vein basining out after another, until the last or bottom vein of the axis runs up on the table land at the end of the mountain, bounded by the conglomerate. The red shale at the termination of the axis, from its soft decomposing nature, forms an abrupt declivity, occasioned by the streams which flow down its sides into the valley below—and this is

---

* Wm. F. Roberts, Esq., Geologist and Mining Engineer, to whom we are indebted for a portion of these remarks on the Geological structure of the coal formation.

the "conspicuous north and south disruption" of Mr. Rogers. Further north than the termination of the first axis, another mountain (not Sharp Mountain,) bounds the south side of the second axis of coal strata of the south anthracite region.

The second synclinal axis lies between the range of hills before named, and a range further north, which, in the vicinity of Pottsville, is called Peach Mountain. The coal veins of the Peach Mountain range are very much contorted in their disposition, having several undulations or axis of a minor synclinal and anticlinal character. In the more elevated land along the range of Peach Mountain, the curvatures of the coal veins are more duplicated than they are in the low parts of this mountain range. A better development of this peculiar coal formation may be seen in the lands north-east of Middleport, where the curvatures of the strata are more numerous and exposed by actual workings, than may be found in any other position along the entire range

The uprising of the coal veins at this place forms several synclinal and anticlinal axis—the lower veins curve over before they reach the surface, and the upper ones lie over them in an uniform way. In some places, where denudation has taken place, the continuity of the saddle, or anticlinal curve of the upper veins, is washed off, and the same veins form several north and south dips, which, previous to the nature of the formation having been clearly understood, were taken for so many different and distinct veins of coal. This misconstruction of the true geological character of the veins, and the reason why so many outcrops are exposed, not being considered, led to a great many errors in the estimation of the real value of the coal land in the Peach Mountain range, as regarded the quantity of mineral contained therein. In many other places, too, in the anthracite formation, the same causes have, and do even at the present time, lead to similar results, and is the reason why erroneous calculations are not unfrequently made.

The extreme length of the axis of Peach Mountain coal strata is about thirty-five miles. The eastern terminus of the synclinal axis is at the Old Summit coal mines on the Lehigh estate. This, the second axis, extends further east than the first axis a distance of about eleven miles. The western extreme point of the second synclinal axis is about twenty-five miles east from the western end of the south fork of coal strata in Dauphin district, and about fourteen miles east from the western end of the north fork of coal strata in Lykens'

Valley district. The point of termination of the second axis is where the two before-named forks begin to diverge in their westward prolongation from their course eastward. The terminus is seven miles north-west from Pinegrove. In the continuation of the axis of Peach Mountain coal strata, the undulations that are found in its central part do not continue through its entire length—as its eastern and western parts—for as the bottom coal veins of the axis become more elevated, the curvatures of the strata are diminished.

The third synclinal axis is between Peach Mountain and Mine Hill, and extends from the point-like terminus of the south anthracite region, near the Lehigh River, to a similar terminus, the end of the north fork in the Lykens' Valley district,—a distance of about fifteen miles. In this axis undulations and curvatures of the coal strata are found, but not of that frequent occurrence as in the Peach Mountain range. These undulations may be seen at Rhume Run, in the Lehigh district; on Silver Creek, in Schuylkill Valley district, (north of Pinegrove,) and in the Lykens' Valley district.

The fourth synclinal axis of coal strata is known as the Broad Mountain coal basin, which lies between Mine Hill and Broad Mountain; its eastern end is between the head waters of Wolf Creek and Silver Creek; its western end is west of "Woolaston's or Raulin's tavern." The length of this axis is about eleven miles.

The fifth synclinal axis of coal strata is on the summit of Broad Mountain; its eastern end is east of New Boston colliery; its western end, west of Raulin's Run. The length of this axis is about fourteen miles. The axis is narrow, and the coal is in places washed off—therefore, it is not so valuable in point of quantity of coal as it would be were the veins continuous through it.

The foregoing axis of coal strata constitute the south anthracite region—the first grand division of the anthracite formation of Pennsylvania.

The middle anthracite region contains, as well as the elongated synclinal and anticlinal axis of coal strata, several small and detached coal basins.

Between Mahanoy Mountain, the south boundary of the middle anthracite region, and the mountain ranging parallel thereto, and next north, known as Locust Mountain, are three synclinal and two anticlinal axis of coal strata. The valley containing these axis is about twenty-six miles in length. The eastern termination of the axis is about eleven miles east from Girardsville, near the head waters of the Mahanoy and source of the tributaries of the Little Schuylkill. The western termination is south of Shamokin. Both terminations of this axis break off in a similar manner to the eastern termination of the first axis, in the south anthracite region. Locust Mountain is the north boundary of the Mahanoy, and the south boundary of Shamokin coal valley. The north boundary of Shamokin coal valley is Big Mountain. In the Shamokin coal valley, taking its central part as a section, there are four synclinal and three anticlinal axis of coal strata, besides a roll of the outcrops of the lower veins of coal shown on the north slope of Locust Mountain. The first synclinal axis of the Shamokin coal valley is between Locust Mountain and Mount Carmel Ridge; the second between Mount Carmel Ridge and Mine Ridge; the third between Mine Ridge and Coal Run Ridge; the fourth between Coal Run Ridge and Big Mountain.

The anticlinal axis are Mount Carmel, Mine Ridge and Coal Run Ridge. The most complete and beautiful development of the coal strata of the anthracite formation of Pennsylvania, is the anticlinal axis of Mount Carmel Ridge, developed by the north branch of Shamokin Creek. The creek passes through the axis at a right angle to the run of the coal strata, about five hundred yards west from the centre turnpike at Mount Carmel—the arch of sandstone rock is cut down perpendicularly, forming a beautiful curve, and giving an admirable illustration of the regularity and perfection of this part of the coal field. The anticlinal axis of Mine Ridge is likewise cut by the same stream, and affords another example of the perfection of the coal strata of the Shamokin coal valley. Mine Ridge, from the Centre turnpike, gradually rises into a hill of great elevation eastward, where coal veins of great thickness and extraordinarily pure quality are opened—a strong evidence that this ridge or axis of coal strata, when thoroughly developed, will prove to contain mineral in quantity and quality inferior to few other places in the anthracite formation of Pennsylvania.

Big Mountain contains the bottom series of coal veins which crop out along its summit. These veins are the same as those developed in Locust Mountain, the thickest veins of the anthracite formation.

The Shamokin coal valley extends in length from its eastern terminus, on the head waters of Little Schuylkill and Quaquake creeks, to its western terminus within about seven miles from the Susquehanna—a distance of about forty miles.

The eastern terminus of the Shamokin coal valley has two forks of coal strata, similar to the forks of the western terminus of the south anthracite region, but much smaller in point of length and width.

North of these forks are the detached coal basins of Beaver Meadow, Dreck Creek, Hazleton, Black Creek, Little Black Creek, Sandy Creek, and Hell Kitchen, extending one after the other northward to the Nescopeck Mountain. The Nescopeck summit is conglomerate, the base of the coal formation; and from it to the Wyoming coal field, traces of the coal formation are found—a sufficient evidence that the three great divisions of the anthracite formation of Pennsylvania were, in former times, a connected and continuous formation of coal strata.

The Black Creek coal basin, laying about one mile and a half north from the Hazleton coal basin collieries, in Luzerne County, has for the last few years been attracting much attention, owing to the extensive explorations made by boring and shafting on the Black Creek coal estate, where a mammoth vein of coal has been struck and passed through, of the thickness of twenty-eight feet, and two other veins, one of six and the other of seven feet. These veins of coal are supposed to underlay the greater part of this estate, and show themselves to be of the very best quality. In fact, it is believed by many that when the Black Creek coal basin shall be fully developed, it will be found one of the richest basins in the Lehigh coal field. This basin, as far as the developments extend, would seem to afford to the miner easy facilities for taking out the coal, and its proximity to the Hazleton Railroad, must in a short time render it of great consideration to those who are now the owners of the land. This basin is about fifteen miles in length, and has many advantages in procuring supplies, such as provisions, &c., being but a short distance from the beautiful farming district of Conyngham Valley, and only separated from it by Buck Mountain.

The south anthracite region contains white, red, and gray ash coal veins. The white ash are found in the Lehigh, the Broad Mountain, the Mine Hill, and underlie the Pottsville basin. The principal gray ash are in the Peach Mountain range, and the principal red ash coal are the south dipping veins of the first synclinal axis. The south fork in Dauphin district has, in its eastern end, a semi-bituminous coal, which gradually changes, going westward, into a pure bituminous. A similar graduated change from an anthracite to a bituminous coal is found in the coal formation of Wales, in Great Britain, and according to Professor Murchison, in several coal fields in Russia the coal veins which are bituminous at one part of the basin, become anthracite at the other. Lykens' Valley district yields coal of a semi-bituminous or free burning quality. Argillaceous iron ore, both nodular and in seams, is found varying with the coal veins in places through the coal region, and black band or carboniferous iron-stone is found in the Lykens' Valley district.

In the middle anthracite region is found white, gray, and red ash coal veins. In Big Mountain a superior vein of red ash coal, seven feet in thickness, which burns very freely and leaves no clinker, is opened with white ash coal veins above and below it. Red ash coal veins are found in other localities in this coal region. Argillaceous iron ore in the nodular form, and in regular strata, appears to be in abundance through this coal region ; and bog ore exists in large beds in various places. Carboniferous iron-stone is likewise found in this region, and may ultimately become an article of great value for smelting purposes.

HISTORY OF MINING OPERATIONS.

SCHUYLKILL DISTRICT.—Like every other branch of business, the mining of coal has undergone many striking changes and improvements, since its commencement. We have frequent cause for astonishment, while regarding the progress of improvement in every department of busy life; and although it would seem, standing upon the platform of the present, and taking in the whole perspective of the past, with its numerous shades, that we have really achieved the *ne plus ultra* of inventive genius ;—still, as the world goes on, new enterprises are opened, new feelings are instilled, and new desires are to be filled :—so that the *field* for thought and scientific knowledge

ANTHRACITE COAL FORMATION. 173

is continually enlarged, and the progress of invention must always be proportionably rapid.

When openings were first made for coal in the vicinity of Pottsville, the shafts were sunk to the depth of from twenty to thirty feet, and the coal hoisted in large vessels, by means of a common windlass. As soon as the water became troublesome, which was usually the case after penetrating beyond thirty feet, the shaft was abandoned, and another sunk, and the same simple process repeated.

This mode, however, was soon superseded by *drifts* (or openings above water-level, running in with a surface sufficiently inclined to drain off the water). These would be opened at the heads of veins upon the hillsides, and the coal brought out in wheel-barrows; but

FIGURE 51.

it was not until 1827 that railways were introduced into mines, and from that period until 1834 drifts were the only mode pursued for mining coal.

In the meantime, various experiments had been made for the use of shafts, the principal one of which was the substitution of horse-power and the gin, for the windlass, by which means the miners could clear the water from the shaft with greater facility, and penetrate somewhat farther down on the veins. But with this great improvement, as it was then regarded, they were enabled to run down on the vein for but a comparatively short distance, and the coal was, of course, inferior; for experience has since demonstrated that the crop of the coal is never equal to that taken out at lower depths, where the roof and floor have attained the regularity and hardness so necessary for effective labor and good coal.

At the period to which we have alluded, there was a total and perfect absence of every convenience which is now deemed necessary for mining operations. The country itself was, we were about to say, *uninviting;* but such we never could have esteemed it. There never *was* a more grand, picturesque region, beautiful at all seasons grand in all eyes, precious to the man of science, the capitalist, and to the whole world of business. But if it be wild and beautiful *now*, when jealous art has despoiled it somewhat of its wild aspect; stripped the mountains of their gaudy foliage, and levelled the venerable and sturdy forest trees to the earth, with here and there a few remaining, stripped of bark and branches, as if intended for monuments to their perished fellows; what must it *not* have been when the howls of wild beasts echoed in the solitary depths of the woods; in the deep ravines and mountain-passes until then unexplored by man? The country then, clothed in its rich spring garb, fragrant with its wild-flowers, musical with its numerous streams, majestic with its frowning crags and precipices, in its general range resembled the green ocean "into tempest tossed," and its primitive silence was the sleep of nature, when, like a miser, she had finished burying her treasures!

But what we wished to convey is, that the country at this period was destitute of those conveniences for sustaining life, and for carrying on a regular business, which are rightfully looked for by the laborer. The only mode of transporting coal from the mine, was by common wagons, over roads at all seasons bad, and through a country in which, from its mountainous character and wild state, the horse was enabled to accomplish but little, in comparison with what could be done in a level and more improved country.

But notwithstanding these difficulties, the work was still pursued, and that most assiduously. The prices commanded by coal afforded but a scanty pittance to the laborers employed, without insuring the least profit to the owner of the lands. Previously, the inhabitants of the country subsisted entirely by their skill in hunting. Every species of game was plenty, and the skins of bears, wolves, wild cats, foxes, &c., as well as the quarters of deers, and birds, were eagerly sought in the country and towns adjacent. The hunters, few in number, lived in rude cabins far from each other, and there was scarcely a path, in the rugged state of the country, by which the steps of the stranger could be directed. All the coal mined anterior to 1818, was mostly sold to blacksmiths in the surrounding country; for to haul it away for fuel, while wood was still plenty, could not be afforded nor justified by the economist.

Although the Schuylkill Navigation, as previously stated, had been completed in 1818, its facilities for transporting coal were not of such character as to warrant the mining of any considerable quantity. Having been thrown out of repair, time after time, by freshets, its use could by no means be relied upon, and thus, from 1818 to 1825, the trade, if it may be said to have had existence at all, was so extremely limited and uncertain in its general features and prospects, that little attention was bestowed upon it. The whole extent of the trade of the anthracite regions, from this period to 1824, did not exceed twenty thousand tons. In 1825, (the year following,) this amount was nearly doubled, of which the quantity sent down the Schuylkill was six thousand five hundred tons; that of the Lehigh twenty-eight thousand one hundred tons, and of the Susquehanna no account has been kept.

From this year, therefore, the existence of the Schuylkill trade may be dated—that of the Lehigh having commenced five years previously.

The introduction of railways into this region, which occurred in 1827, is, perhaps, one of the most important epochs in its history. The natural arrangement of the country is admirably adapted for grading and laying down railways, and it was on this account that their introduction was more welcome. The coal seams crop out by the sides of the mountains, and the valleys between them, usually affording small streams, allow sufficient descent to convey the loaded cars to the head of navigation. The distinguished credit of having been the first person who erected a railway in this region, is, we believe, assigned to the late Abraham Pott, who constructed one over half a mile in length, leading from his mines, east of Port Carbon, to the navigation at that place.

Their subsequent introduction into drifts, by which the cars were drawn in the mines by mules, gave a new impulse to the business, and greatly added to the capacity of each operator. In 1826 the amount shipped was nearly seventeen thousand tons, and in 1827 it was over thirty-one thousand tons. In 1828 it reached forty-seven thousand, in 1829 seventy-nine thousand, 1830 eighty-nine thousand, and in 1831 eighty-one thousand tons.

During this period coal was being generally used in stoves, in the more populous towns; and after the grate was introduced into them, which was accomplished more or less successfully between the years 1827 and 1831, the trade began to assume an imposing and gigantic attitude. For no sooner had the people become familiar with the peculiar properties of the coal, than its vast future importance in the arts and manufactures was readily acknowledged.

In 1826 and '27 large accessions had been made to the population and business of the region. The Schuylkill Navigation had been placed in excellent repair, and interruptions in its navigation were no longer experienced. This happy state of affairs continued until 1829, when a momentary pause was made in the trade, but it was a pause prophetic only of still greater triumphs, of busier scenes, and of more active life. It was at this period that scenes of excitement, speculation, and daring enterprise were enacted, which surprised and startled our good old Commonwealth from its Quaker propriety. Capitalists awoke, as if from a dream, and wondered that they had never before realized the importance of the anthracite trade! What appeared yesterday but as a fly, now assumed the gigantic proportions of an elephant! The capitalist who, but a few years previously, laughed at the *infatuation* of the daring pioneers of the coal trade, now coolly ransacked his papers, and cyphered out his available means, and whenever met on the street, his hand and pockets would be filled with plans of towns, of surveys of coal lands, and calculations and specifications of railways, canals, and divers other improvements until now unheard of! The land which yesterday would not have commanded the taxes levied upon it, was now looked upon as "dearer than Plutarch's mine, richer than gold." Sales were made to a large amount, and in an incredibly short space of time, it is estimated that upwards of *five millions of dollars* had been invested in lands in the Schuylkill coal field alone! Laborers and mechanics of all kinds, and from all quarters and nations, flocked to the coal region, and found ready and constant employment at the most exorbitant wages. Capitalists, arm-in-arm with confidential advisers, civil engineers, and grave scientific gentlemen, explored every recess, and solemnly contemplated the present and future value and importance of each particular spot. Houses could not be built fast enough, for where nought but bushes and rubbish were seen one day, a smiling village would be discovered on the morrow. Enterprising carpenters in Philadelphia, and elsewhere along the line of canal, prepared the timber and frame-work of houses, and then placing the *material* on board a canal boat, would hasten on to the enchanted spot to dedicate it to its future purposes. Thus *whole towns* were arriving in the returning canal boats, and as "they were forced to play the owl," a moonlight night was a god-send to the impatient proprietors, for with the dawning of the morning would be reflected the future glory of the new town, and the restless visages of scores of anxious lessees!

The days of speculation, however, were not terminated in '29; and a few words more remain to be said concerning them. Many persons who had purchased lands, moved thither with their families, designing to take up their permanent abode in the region, and pursue the mining business regularly, as they would farming, or any other calling. But, in a majority of cases, the lands were purchased in large tracts, by companies formed for the purpose, and these, as well as many tracts held by single individuals, were leased out to tenants. These joint-stock companies, or those composed of citizens of other States, obtained charters for the mining of coal from the Legislatures of their respective States, and thus evaded the statutes of *mortmain* in force here; and the lands owned by them were held by deeds of trust, and were thus used and occupied. But no sooner were companies chartered by the Legislature of this State, than a general law was passed escheating the lands of companies formed under charters not granted by this State, and held without its license and consent. This was done in 1833, when the trade had partially recovered from the speculations of the previous years.

It was under such circumstances as these that a vast amount of capital had been expended in the region, not only in the improvement of the lands, and the facilities for mining coal, but in the construction of railways and similar improvements, of the most stupendous character.

In contemplating these times, though we cannot but laugh at the ludicrous scenes they present, all will admit that they were the indirect and direct means of accomplishing incalculable benefit to the whole country. Nor was it possible, under the circumstances, to restrain the fever of speculation. The real value and resources of the lands were comparatively unknown, and in the hands of those who had no intention of "piercing the bowels of the earth, and bringing forth from the caverns of mountains treasures which shall give strength to our hands, and subject all nature to our use and pleasure," a fictitious value could not but be placed upon them. Calculations were cunningly made of the number of *square yards of coal* in an acre, and the quantity each acre was capable of yielding, without considering the labor and expense necessary to mine it, or without knowing in fact that it contained coal at all, and exhibiting such calculations, in glaring and *bona fide* figures, to the bewildered capitalists, land would sell for one hundred dollars an acre to-day; to-morrow for three hundred, and then for five hundred dollars. And when, at last, the tracts were cut up into small parcels, to suit the means of the purchaser, they would presently be esteemed as beautiful locations for towns, and straightway plans were laid out on paper, elegantly printed and colored; and, finally, the whole would wind up with a sale of "valuable town lots"—lying, perhaps, in the heart of a swamp, a forest, or upon the brow of a mountain. This *last* operation would frequently prove the "noblest Roman of them all;" for although the purchaser might have paid five hundred dollars per acre for the whole plot, he would realize the whole of that sum on a single "corner-lot," and if he could make five or six hundred lots, there would be no such thing as estimating his profits!

We shall dismiss this subject with a single remark. The speculating mania had involved hundreds of persons in utter ruin; and there were few persons of fortune who now ventured, voluntarily and alone, into the mining business. Companies were formed, not only for the purchase of the lands, but also for conducting mining operations upon them; and it was thus hoped, that by concentrating the lands and business of the region into the hands of a few, whose combined capital and influence could silence individual competition, the trade could be made obedient to their wild schemes. Coal had already been universally adopted; and by withholding supplies when they were absolutely needed, it was thought that it could be made to command from eight to twelve dollars a ton; and then, the price being thus established, another series of "calculations" of the value of each particular acre of coal land, and fresh ground for speculations, would be laid open. Advocates for coal companies were consequently not lacking, and many were chartered by the Legislature. But the practical experience of those interested in the trade soon awakened a powerful opposition to them, and this feeling has existed from very nearly the commencement of the trade to the present time. It was especially active from 1831 to 1839, during which the trade had thrice fallen off, in the gross amount of the annual product, from the years respectively preceding; and during the whole of which period, the influence of the public journals in the coal regions was directly arrayed against them. The country, through such aid, was happily saved from the calamities which threatened the trade, and which did much, during this period, to retard its annual growth.

ANTHRACITE FOR SMELTING IRON.

Nothing worthy of special notice occurred in the progress of the anthracite trade, until 1838, 1839, and 1840. It was during this period, that the attention of intelligent and enterprising citizens was called to the practicability of using anthracite coal for the smelting of iron ore. Dr. Weisenheimer, of New York, had, in the latter part of 1838, and before similar results had been obtained, or at least promulgated in Europe, secured a patent for smelting iron with anthracite and hot blast; but Mr. Crane, having about this time succeeded in a series of experiments in Wales, having in view the same object, is understood to have purchased the claims of Dr. W., which were as follows: *First:* In the application of anthracite coal, exclusively or in part, for deoxidating and carbonating iron ore. *Second:* The application of anthracite coal, exclusively or in part, in combining iron in a metallic state, with a greater quantity of carbon; if bar-iron, for steel; if pig or cast-iron, for a superior quality, &c. *Third:* The smelting or reducing of iron-ore, so deoxidated and carbonated by the application of anthracite coal as aforesaid, into pig or cast-iron. *Fourth:* The refining or converting of iron ore, so deoxidated or carbonated by the application of anthracite coal, as aforesaid, into malleable or bar iron. *Fifth:* The application of anthracite coal as a fuel, in smelting or reducing iron ore raw or roasted, but not prepared by a separate process of deoxidation and carbonation, as above described, into pig or cast iron. *Sixth:* Though not claiming an exclusive right of the use of heated air for any kind of fuel, nevertheless he claimed the use of heated air, applied upon and in connection with the said principle and method discovered by him to smelt iron ore in blast furnaces, with anthracite coal, by applying a blast of air in such quantity, velocity and density, or under such pressure as the compactness or density, and the continuity of the anthracite coal requires, as above described, &c.

As soon as this transfer was effected, Mr. Crane obtained a patent in this country, which differed slightly from Dr. W.'s. But it was several months anterior to the dates of both these patents that a furnace had been blown in at Mauch Chunk, which used anthracite as fuel, and this enterprise was followed in a short time after by a more extensive and successful one at Pottsville. In consequence of this, and in view of the certainty of litigation, Mr. Crane never insisted upon an observance of his claims by priority of discovery, but, as we are informed, published a card, formally renouncing them.

Experiments for using anthracite coal in blast furnaces had been made at Mauch Chunk in 1830, by the Lehigh coal company; and up to the period of

Mr. Crane's method, vast sums of money had been expended, from time to time, in different parts of Europe, to effect the same object, but every attempt proved unsuccessful. The thing had been almost entirely abandoned as impracticable, when the great secret seems to have been imparted simultaneously in Europe and America—for while Mr. Crane was rejoicing over his triumphs in Wales, three enterprising gentlemen of Reading were repairing and blowing in their furnace at Mauch Chunk—and if not the very one previously abandoned, it was the ground, at least, which had sustained a former defeat!

From a letter, by Mr. Lawthrop, dated at Beaver Meadows, to Prof. Walter R. Johnson, of Philadelphia, we gather the following interesting particulars concerning this first application of anthracite coal for smelting purposes: The experiments, says Mr. L., were made by Messrs. Joseph Baughman, Julius Guiteau and Henry High, of Reading, in an old furnace which was temporarily fitted up for the purpose. They used about eight per cent. of anthracite, and the result was such as to surprise those who witnessed it, (for it was considered as an impossibility, even by iron masters,) and amply sufficient to encourage those engaged in it to go on. In order, therefore, to test the matter more thoroughly, they built a furnace on a small scale, near the Mauch Chunk weighlock, which was completed during the month of July, 1839. The dimensions, &c., were as follows: stack, $21\frac{1}{2}$ feet high, 22 feet square at the base; boshes, $5\frac{1}{2}$ feet across; hearth, 14 by 16 inches in the square, and 4 feet by 9 inches from the dam stone to the back. The blowing apparatus consisted of 2 cylinders, each 6 feet diameter; a receiver, same diameter, and about $2\frac{1}{2}$ feet deep; stroke 11 inches—each piston making from 12 to 15 strokes per minute. An overshot water-wheel, diameter 14 feet: length of bucket, $3\frac{1}{2}$ feet; number of buckets, 36; revolutions per minute, from 12 to 15.

The blast was applied August 27th, and the furnace kept in blast until September 10th, when they were obliged to stop in consequence of the apparatus for heating the blast proving to be too temporary. Several tons of iron were produced of Nos. 2 and 3 quality. Temperature of the blast did not exceed 200° Fahrenheit—the proportion of anthracite used not remembered.

A new and good apparatus for heating the blast was next procured, (at which time Mr. Lowthrop became personally interested in the works,) consisting of 200 feet in length, of cast iron pipes, $1\frac{1}{2}$ inches thick; it was placed in a brick chamber, at the runnel head, and heated by a flame issuing thence.

The blast was again applied about the last of November, 1839, and the furnace worked remarkably well for five weeks, exclusively with anthracite coal; they were then obliged, for want of ore, to blow out on the 12th of January, 1839. During this experiment, says Mr. L., our doors were open to the public, and we were watched very closely both night and day—for men could hardly believe what they saw with their own eyes, so incredulous was the public in regard to the matter at that time. Some iron masters expressed themselves astonished, that a furnace *could work* whilst using unburnt, unwashed, frozen ore, such as was put into our furnace. The amount of iron produced was about $1\frac{1}{2}$ tons per day, when working best, of Nos. 1, 2, and 3 quality—the temperature of the blast being still about 400° Fahrenheit.

The following season the hearth was enlarged to 19 by 21 inches, and 5 feet 3 inches from the dam stone to the back of hearth; and on July 26th, the furnace was again put in blast, and continued in blast until December, 1840, a few days after the dissolution of the firm, when it was blown out in good order. For about three months no other kind than anthracite was used, and the product was about 100 tons of iron, good Nos. 1, 2, and 3 quality. When working best, the furnace produced about two tons per day. Temperature of the blast was from 400 to 600° Fahrenheit.

The following ores were used: "pipe" ore, from Miller's mine, near Allentown; "brown hematite," commonly called *top mine*, or iron-face ore; "rock" ore, from Dickerson's mine, in New Jersey; and "Williams township" ore, in Northampton county. The last mentioned ore produced a very strong iron, and when it is considered that these experiments were conducted under circumstances wholly unfavorable, and that the furnace and machinery were thoroughly defective, the results obtained may be viewed as being in the highest degree satisfactory.

In December, 1840, this furnace was blown out, the work discontinued, and the firm dissolved. The furnace at Pottsville having at this time been in operation, and its performances having been decidedly superior, the credit of first *successfully* introducing anthracite coal for smelting purposes has been very justly claimed by the citizens of that place. For although the furnace at Mauch Chunk had overcome many difficulties, its abandonment so soon was by many regarded as *prima facia* evidence of failure—while the other has continued in operation, with short intervals, to a very recent period. It is still standing, and under a favorable aspect of the iron market, might probably be again worked with profit.

The Pottsville furnace was completed, and put in blast on the 26th of October, 1839, under the direction of the celebrated Mr. Perry. This gentleman, who had frequently visited Mr. Crane in Wales, and was familiar with the process adopted by him, declared that the performances of this furnace more than equalled those obtained by that gentleman. They were, therefore, esteemed as in the highest degree successful, and an intelligent iron master, (Hon. Dr. Eckert,) who had observed its workings, declared that it had triumphed over difficulties and accidents, during the first fortnight of its existence, which would have chilled up any charcoal works over and over again! The hearth was tapped night and morning, and the yield at each time varied from sixty to sixty-three pigs, equal to about three tons of metal. It is an all-important fact, that in charging the stack, nothing but pure anthracite coal and iron ore was used. Not a scrap of old metal, wood or charcoal was used, except for the mere purpose of first ignition.

The erection of this furnace was mainly accomplished through the efforts of Burd Patterson, Esq., who, from the earliest history of this region, has been identified with every measure of its onward progress. He is still a resident of Pottsville, and, as heretofore, stands connected with all new and praiseworthy enterprises.

In January, 1840, the furnace having now performed successfully for three months, a deputation, consisting of the late Nicholas Biddle, Thomas Biddle, Isaac Lea, Jesse Richards, J. M. Sanderson, and Dr. B. Kugler, visited Pottsville to inspect the iron-works, and to award a prize of five thousand dollars, subscribed by certain influential citizens of Pennsylvania, to be presented to the individual who would, within a specified time, succeed in smelting a certain amount of iron ore, with anthracite coal, &c. This prize was accordingly awarded to the proprietor of the Pottsville furnace, and therefore settles the question as to the person and place entitled to the credit of having first succeeded in this important enterprise.

The celebration of this event was a happy and brilliant affair, and it was not long ere the Union was filled with the importance of the achievement thus commemorated. The committee were invited to a dinner at the Mount Carbon House, and a toast, complimental to the distinguished gentlemen composing it, having been offered, Mr. N. Biddle responded to it in behalf of his colleagues, in a speech of great practical learning and profound eloquence, at the conclusion of which he offered the following toast:

"*Old Pennsylvania*—Her sons, like her soil, a rough outside, but solid stuff within; plenty of coal to warm her friends, plenty of iron to cool her enemies."

The Pottsville Furnace was soon followed by another in the vicinity, called the Valley Furnace. This was put in blast, September 17, 1841, and "succeeded admirably from the first moment of its action." It used the ore found upon the ground.

At the latter end of 1842, after the passage of the tariff act of that year, anthracite furnaces began very rapidly to multiply. In the following year they were found in full blast, and others going into operation, in almost every county in the State, where coal and iron ore were at all accessible. The number continued annually to increase, at an astonishing rate, until the passage of the present tariff law, which has thus far had a very disastrous effect upon this branch of American industry. It will not be long, however, before we recover all the strength that has been lost or impaired during the last few years, for such is the enterprise of our citizens that they *will* produce, notwithstanding the competition of their British rivals.

Until the year 1740, iron was made in England almost exclusively with charcoal, and prior to that period none of the iron stones of the coal region were used; but as soon as the iron manufacturers found it necessary to locate themselves in the coal region for the purpose of being convenient to the new kind of fuel they were about to adopt, they found the necessity of searching for ore nearer their works than the magnetic ores that they had been in the habit of using were; the result was, that an abundance of excellent ore was discovered in the coal regions in the immediate vicinity of their works, and although it did not yield so high a per centage of iron as the magnetic ores, they found it more profitable than transporting richer ores from a distance.

With regard to this region, a like result has been experienced; for it was not until after the erection of the furnace at this place, that any investigations had been instituted as to whether iron ore was to be obtained or not. But no sooner had explorations commenced than new and large deposits of iron ore were found daily, and the ore pronounced to be of an excellent quality. Mr. Benj. Perry, the intelligent anthracite founder, has visited several of these mines, and gave it as his opinion that any number of furnaces could be supplied with ore for an indefinite time.

In comparing the ores of this country with those of England and Wales, we find the average richness to be nearly the same; but we have a decided and important advantage in the thickness of the veins, many of which being upwards of three feet thick, and from that down to six inches. The average richness of the ores taken from the coal regions of England and Wales, is about 33 per cent. The average richness of eight specimens of ore, taken from the Pottsville coal region, was 33·18 of metallic ore. These specimens were analysed under the direction of Prof. Rogers, late State Geologist—some of them yielding 39, 38, and 37 per cent., and all taken from different veins. Prof. R. in his fourth annual report to the Legislature of this State, speaking of these ores, says: "Especial care has been taken to submit to chemical examination, such specimens *only* as represent the *average* character of their respective beds—choosing those freshly opened in the mines, or in some deep excavation, and *rejecting*, as far as possible, samples gathered from the outcrop, or found loose on the surface; as they invariably contain too high a per centage to prove a fair criterion," &c.

The presence of inexhaustible supplies of coal and iron ore, suggests an important advantage in the comparatively limited capital necessary to carry on iron works. For while iron masters in other sections of country are compelled, at all seasons, to keep on hand a large supply of coal and ore, no such necessity would exist here. Supplies could be procured in small quantities, as desired, for immediate use, and the necessity of buying large quantities at *high prices*, is thus entirely overcome. The same argument holds good, as regards means of transportation, and speedy and cheap access to market. While iron works at many places have no avenue to market during the winter, and are consequently compelled to retain a large stock of their manufactured product on hand—the manufacturer here could send it to market in such quantities, and at such times as the demand might justify.

We may next consider the *cheapness* of the fuel, as well as of the ores used. For the former, the fine refuse coal that has been crowding our mines and landings for years past, is now brought into use for generating steam and heating the blast, and besides answering admirably the purpose, it is afforded free of charge, and delivered to the furnace by the coal operators, so anxious are they to get rid of the large quantities annually accumulated about their premises. This, it will be granted, is an important consideration.

There is another consideration, with regard to those locations where the advantages, in some instances, consist merely or principally in being in the immediate vicinity of the ore. After the smelting of the ore into pig metal is accomplished, no more ore is required; but in the process of making bar-iron, about *four tons of coal* are necessary to manufacture one ton of the latter, so that, independent of the saving in the cost of making pig metal in the coal region, the saving in converting it into bar-iron, at a large rolling mill, would be immense.

The middle anthracite region, as we are assured by our friend, William F. Roberts, holds out inducements of the most favorable character for the investment of capital, in all the branches of iron making and iron manufactures. The coal is of superior quality, and may be mined at very low rates. Its iron ore is rich and in abundance, while it has other important facilities for iron-making establishments to operate with the greatest economy and profit.

The lands of the Dauphin Coal Company, we may add, are also admirably calculated to sustain extensive iron establishments. Taking in view the admirable outlets to market, and the peculiar character of the coal, and richness of the iron ore, they may be said to enjoy unequalled advantages for this branch of manufactures.

PROCESSES OF MINING COAL.

We shall now resume the subject of mining, and briefly allude to some of the principal improvements lately introduced.

After the introduction of railways, there seems to have been little done in the way of improvements, to facilitate the operation of mining. But without tracing, in regular order, the introduction of each new feature, as the present is contradistinguished from the past, we shall at once proceed to explain the *modus operandi* of mining, as observed in the present day.

In the first place, it may be necessary to premise that the *range* of all the coal veins in the Schuylkill basin is east and west, converging to the eastward, and diverging westward, with such slight variation from the general rule, as not to be worthy of notice. The *dip* of the veins is to the south: and their angle of inclination from the horizon varies from 30° to 40° parallel, in all cases, with the surrounding strata. From 1833 the number of operations below water-level has annually increased, in a regular per centage with the increase of the trade. As they are the most extensive, and would, perhaps, prove most interesting to the stranger, we shall now describe the minutiæ of which they are comprised.

FIG. 52.—VIEW OF A COAL SLOPE.

When a vein of coal is being worked below water-level, a steam-engine and pumps are necessary to raise up the accumulated water in the mine; for *below* water-level means, simply, that the coal is being mined at some point *below* the bed of the adjacent river, creek, or rivulet. The first step to be taken at the commencement of an operation of this kind, is to ascertain where the vein *crops out* to the surface, or so near to the surface as to be easily found, from a previous knowledge of the range of the vein. A favorable location must then be selected, twenty or thirty feet to the northward of the crop of the vein, for the location of a stationary steam-engine. This must be where a sufficiency of water can be had for the supply of the steam-boilers; and if not near to a main railroad, prudence will dictate that it must be so situated that a branch or lateral road can be laid down near the place where the engine is to be erected. The descent into the mine is called a *Slope*, and thus those mines below water-level, called *Slopes*, are contradistinguished from those above water-level, called *Drifts*. Engines erected for the purpose of hoisting the coal up the Slope, and pumping the water out of the mine, are usually of the capacity of from forty, fifty, and sixty horse-power, nearly all horizontal high-pressure, and working with a slide-valve. They are generally built in a very neat, simple, as well as a strong and efficient manner, and invariably by the mechanics of the coal region.

The location of the engine being determined upon, a slope, or inclined plane, must be driven down in the vein, and consequently at the same angle of inclination. The thickness of the vein is usually excavated, and the slope must be sufficiently wide to admit of two railway tracks, from thirty-six to forty inches wide each, to be laid down; with room, also, for the pumps on one side, (and sometimes both sides) and travelling road on the other side (or sometimes *between*

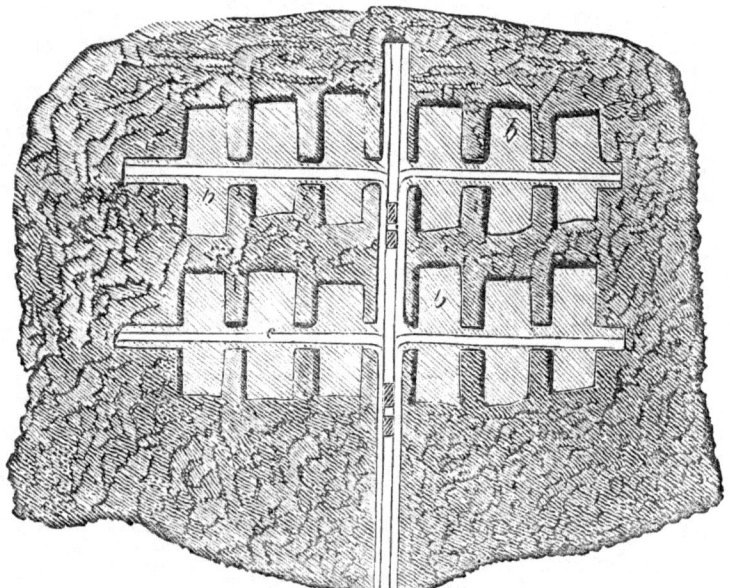

FIG. 53.—GROUND-PLAN OF A COAL MINE.

the two railway tracks) for the miners and laborers—the whole width of the slope being usually from eighteen to twenty-two feet. The slope is driven down about two hundred feet for the *first level*, at the bottom of which the *gangways* are commenced, running at right-angles from the slope, east and west in the vein, and are continued at distances discretionary with the operator, or to the extremity of his mining limits. The slope and gangways form a capital T. The gangways are frequently driven one, two, or three miles, with turnouts at intervals for trains to pass each other. They are made about seven feet high, and sufficiently wide to admit a railroad track to be laid down, on which a well loaded car, having from one to two tons of coal, may pass freely. (Fig. 53. The gangways are indicated by the letter c, on the left.) The cars are hauled to and fro by horses or mules; the latter being preferred, as well because of their diminutive size as for their stamina. The gangways being driven in a sufficient distance from the bottom of the slope, the next thing is to commence digging out or *mining the coal.* The coal in the vein is left undisturbed on each side of the slope to a distance of thirty or forty feet east and west, and extending all the way up the surface; the coal thus left, in mining phraseology, is called *pillars*, and is suffered to remain for the purpose of strengthening or supporting the slope; as in an extensive mine and in a good vein its use may be required for a great number of years. A *pillar* of coal of some twenty feet in width is also left all along the upper side of the gangway; and above this pillar, and up to the surface, all the coal is worked out. The plan of working adopted by miners is this: two miners and a laborer generally work a-breast, (the excavated squares, indicated by the letter b, are breasts where the coal is being worked out,) like the swarth of a *cradler* in the harvest field, usually from thirty to forty feet in width from the pillar above the gangway up to the surface. They make an opening from the gangway through the pillar above, about where the centre of the breast will be, of four or five feet wide, for a *shute ;* after which the full extent of the breast is opened out, and the shute continued up the centre, down which the coal slides into a car in the gangway. When the coal is dug out, the roof is supported by *props of timber*, placed at a distance from each other, varying from six to eight or ten feet, as the roof may be found to be substantial or indifferent. The seams of coal vary from two to twenty-five feet in thickness, (rarely exceeding the latter figure). Those of from six to ten feet are considered best, as they can be worked with greater facility and profit. They can be so propped and roofed as to enable the miner to take out every particle of coal, without the slightest danger of accident; while those of greater thickness must be worked in *chambers*, and large *pillars of coal* left standing to support the roof; and even then the miner is exposed to danger from the detached pieces falling down continually.

From ten to fifty of these breasts are worked simultaneously up to the surface; after which, if the gangway is far enough extended, new ones are commenced, and the same operation repeated, until all the coal on that *level* is worked out. When this is done, the slope must again be driven down some two or three hundred feet; gangways again opened, railways laid down, and the same process of mining the coal continued. And thus the miner gradually gets deeper and deeper into the bowels of the earth, and to reward his industry and perseverance, nature has provided the purest and best coal low down, so that the farther down he ventures, the better and richer becomes his reward!

The deeper the mine, however, the more difficulty is experienced in keeping the works properly supplied with fresh and wholesome air; and nothing but long practical experience can furnish a thorough knowledge of this very important branch of the mining business. We shall reserve some remarks which we intend to offer on this subject, for the conclusion of the present article.

Going now to the shutes in the gangway, we find cars loaded with coal. A mule, which is in most cases used, will draw three or four of these loaded cars to the foot of the slope, where they are left, and empty cars hauled back to be loaded. One of the loaded cars is then pushed upon a turning platform, by a person stationed there for that purpose; he places the car fairly for the railroad track in the slope, attaches the chain to it, draws the pull of the bell as a signal to inform those above that "all is ready," and it is hoisted up the slope by the engine, while an empty car descends, at the same time, on the other track. The car of coal being now brought to the top, it is unhitched, pushed aside, and an empty car pushed into its place, hooked to the chain, and, a loaded car being now attached on the *other* track, the bell is again rung, and the empty car descends and the loaded one ascends, as before. This hoisting and lowering of cars is always going on with despatch during the day-time, and sometimes during the whole night, there being often two sets of hands and miners, one for the day and the other for the night. The time usually occupied for bringing up a car is about one minute, which includes attaching to and detaching the car from the chain, &c. Where from one to two hundred tons of coal are prepared and shipped daily, (besides the

ANTHRACITE COAL FORMATION.   189

refuse and accumulated rubbish of the mine, which must be brought up.) it will be seen that it forms one of the most important features in mining.

The next feature in mining is that of preparing the coal for market, that is, cleaning it from the slate and earthy matter that sometimes is mixed with it, and breaking it in suitable sizes for the various purposes required. The coal dirt, consisting of small particles of coal

FIG. 54.—COAL BREAKER.

and slate, besides various kinds of earthy matter excavated in the mine, is hauled out and deposited in heaps along the sides of the hills, where it sometimes forms large elevations. The loaded coal cars, which are here represented as coming from a drift, or a mine above water-level, are seen on the left, running, by a slight inclination, to the Coal Breaker, which is represented in fig. 54. To fully retain the *idea*, the loaded cars are seen coming out of the mine, and going directly to the Breaker works. The Breaker machinery is, of course, erected as near to the mouth of the mine as local circumstances will admit, and considerable elevation is necessary in order to break and prepare the coal at as little expense as possible. The side of a hill is therefore preferred, as a railroad to conduct the coal from the mouth of the mine to the Breaker can easily be constructed, and will thus avoid the expense of ropes for an inclined-plane, upon which to haul up the loaded cars.

The Breakers are all turned by steam, with but a few exceptions, where water is at hand. An engine of twelve or fifteen horse-power is requisite for driving the Breaker, and turning the circular screens, and they are built on the same plan as the larger engines used at Slopes for hoisting up the cars and pumping out the water. The Breaker-rollers are of cast-iron, placed in very strong, compact framework, and turned by means of a leather belt and gearing-wheels. The most approved rollers are those perforated between the teeth, being an improvement on the former solid periphery-rollers originally invented, inasmuch as there is thus less solid surface presented to the coal in breaking, and, consequently, less *crushing* and wastage of the coal. The loaded car being brought to the head of the Breaker, it is *dumped*, and the coal falls into a small shute, from which it flows into the Breaker. The coal thus passes between the revolving rollers, whose *projecting teeth* break it into pieces of all sizes. From the rollers, the broken coal falls into screens, which also revolve, and having four or five sections of net-work of different sizes, the different sizes of the coal are thus assorted, falling out of the interstices of the screen into shutes below, which are indicated in fig. 54, as hanging directly over the cars. The coal screen was one of the most important inventions of the day. Previously to the introduction of Breakers, the coal was screened by hand. The screen was from 5 to 8 feet long, and from $1\frac{3}{4}$ to $2\frac{1}{2}$ feet in diameter, and placed in a frame, slightly inclined. As the coal entered the more elevated end, the screen was turned round by hand, like a grindstone. When Breakers were introduced, the screens, as previously, were constructed of bar iron, riveted on frame work. But great trouble and expense were experienced, from their liability to break, and the difficulty of repairing them, the whole work being necessarily stopped until this was accomplished. Attention was soon attracted to the subject, and it was not long ere mechanical ingenuity suggested a remedy. A machine was invented by a citizen of Pottsville, by which the largest and thickest wire is wrought into shape suitable for weaving, which is done by very heavy and improved machinery. Wire as thick as an ordinary ram-rod is crimped by this process, which merely consists of a heavy hammer, suspended in frame-work, which is made to fall upon the wire, placed under it, upon a surface allowing it to receive the particular *bend* desired, after which it is woven into frames of about three feet square. These frames are then placed over a large wooden cylinder, and rounded, when two or more sections are pointed and riveted together, which completes their circular form. The screen, thus complete, is removed from the bench, and joined with another of the same dimensions, but of larger or smaller net-work. These screens are remarkably durable, and are not the least feature which has tended to bring coal Breakers into universal use.

This process for crimping thick iron wire has introduced several new and important objects of manufacture, such as iron wire portable bedsteads, fences and ornamental railings, chairs, sofas, &c.

FIG. 55.—IRON RAILING.

Walker & Son, at the corner of Sixth and Market streets, Philadelphia, have a very extensive establishment exclusively devoted to the production of these articles, which, at no distant day, will supersede most of the same articles now made of wood.

After the coal leaves the screen and falls into its appropriate shutes, railroad cars are hauled immediately along side the openings, which, being raised up like the wickets in a mill dam, the coal falls out into the car, and when a sufficient quantity is obtained, the shute is closed, and then the coal leaves forever the scenes of its past history, and is borne off to its future destiny.

The size of chain generally used for hoisting coal is three-fourths and seven-eighths of an inch; formerly smaller chains were used, and, in fact, smaller engines and lighter machinery; but long experience and heavy bills of repairs have taught the coal operators that engines, pumps, gearings, chains, &c., must be strong and substantial in order to withstand the incessant lifting and straining to which they are subjected.

We may now offer a few remarks in regard to drainage, and the plan of pumping the water out of mines. The capacity of the pump varies from ten or twelve to fourteen inches. The working barrel is placed a little above the turning platform at the bottom of the slope, from which pipes are connected up to the surface, or near enough to the surface to have the water carried off. Pump rods are attached to the bucket in the working-barrel, and extend, of course, to the top of the slope, and are connected, by means of a large pump-wheel, with the engine. Below the working-barrel of the pump, and below the turning platform at the foot of the slope, a *sump* is driven down, of the same dimensions as the slope, to the depth of thirty or more feet. This forms a basin into which the water of the mine collects from all the gangways and turnouts, and when the amount of water in the mine is not very great, it will be a considerable time in filling, during which there need, of course, be no pumping. In rainy seasons the water is sometimes rendered very troublesome in the mines, and it is therefore expedient to have the sump, and all connected with the pumping apparatus, in good order and constant readiness. Pipes are attached below the working-barrel and into the sump, and a connection being thus formed, the water is pumped out. The water is generally pumped out at times when the engine is not hoisting coal, though it is often necessary, however, to hoist and pump at the same time. At some of the collieries two engines are used, one for hoisting up the coal, and the other for pumping up the water. Several hogsheads of water are thrown up per minute, with great ease and regularity.

DRIFTS.—In working a coal mine above water-level, no engine or pumps are required. The drift is commenced on the surface, at the foot of a hill, where the vein crops out, and is driven through the vein in the same manner as described when below water-level. The mine being far enough in, gangways are extended to the right and left, and the coal worked out upon the same plan as in slopes, when it is hauled to the breaker by horses and mules. As the gangway is above water-level, with a slight inclination towards the drift, of course the water will run out, thereby rendering engines, pumps, and pumping apparatus, wholly unnecessary. The mines, both of drifts and slopes, are substantially propped up with timber, indicated in the annexed figure, 56, at a, b, and f, f, f, f, which are the *slabs* of boards; d indicating the groove or canal through which the water flows out.

Blasting is frequently resorted to in mining, especially when working large veins. For this purpose the *safety-fuse* is used almost invariably, the coal being generally so wet and damp that the ordinary processes of blasting would not answer, even if preferable in an

ANTHRACITE COAL FORMATION. 193

FIG. 56.—VIEW OF THE TIMBER OF A DRIFT OR COAL MINE.

economical view, which they are not. The safety-fuse, too, is perfectly safe, which gives it not the least important advantage. It is a species of fire-cracker or cartridge, the principal part of the composition being powder, which is surrounded by a hempen fabric, and then covered with another composition, to render it water-proof, of which the greater part is pitch. In blasting coal it is difficult to keep the water from filling up the drill-hole, but by inserting a piece of safety-fuse, and then fastening it tightly, no other preparations are necessary. The match is applied, and following the powder through the fuse, produces the desired result, affording ample time for the miners to withdraw, whenever desirable.

The anthracite coal fields are, throughout, more or less faulty; the southern region more especially. The seams of coal having been heaved up, and at other places sunk down, their local positions, if we may so say, are very much, and in various ways, disturbed and contorted. A vein of coal may be followed for half a mile, when, gradually or directly, it is found to run out, and a mass of solid rock occupying its place, and rising up immediately *through it*. To get on the vein again, this rock must be tunnelled at an expense varying from ten to thirty dollars per yard, and without knowing, positively, how far the tunnel must be extended ere the end can be accomplished. In cases like this fortunes have been and are annually spent. Persons who have engaged in the mining business, and invested large sums in the erection of the necessary buildings, machinery, railways, etc., after getting fairly into operation, and while their success seemed complete, have struck these faults, and in a short time have been thrown into utter bankruptcy. All their machinery is rendered comparatively idle, their regular business suddenly checked and deranged, and thousands of dollars going out of their pockets. Impressed with the belief, which seems to be invariable in such cases, that a few yards of tunnelling will again place them on the vein, they labor assiduously from day to day, and from week to week, entirely realizing, though not in the literal sense, the lines of Pope:

>Hope springs eternal in the human breast;
>Man never is, but always to be blest!

There are, as we have said, various kinds of faults; in fact, although they may all have been produced by the same general agency, they vary in their particular character according to the different positions previously occupied by the strata. At some places a stratum of clay, or a combination of earthy substances, is interposed; while at others no such obstacles appear, but the vein is broken off, and the dismembered portion *sunk down*, just as we can suppose a piece of glass, laying on several small rollers, and then suddenly broken into irregular fragments; some pieces would be comparatively large, some would no doubt nearly and quite join each other, while others would occupy various relative positions to the mass.

The reader will agree with us that coal mining, under such circumstances, cannot but be an extremely hazardous and uncertain business; and, indeed, the experience of some of our most enterprising and intelligent operators affords substantial proof of the fact. There is no such thing as overcoming or avoiding, entirely, even with the best practical experience, the difficulties and dangers with which it is fraught.

IMPORTANT WORK ON PENNSYLVANIA.

To all who are interested in the Pennsylvania Railroad Company, in the Reading Railroad Company, and in the Norristown, and other Railroad Companies in the State; in the Schuylkill and Lehigh Navigation Companies; in the Lehigh, and all other Coal Companies throughout Pennsylvania; to all engaged in Mining and Manufacturing Coal and Iron; to every Farmer and every Citizen of the great State of Pennsylvania, the following important Work, on THE STATE; ITS RESOURCES, IMPROVEMENTS, AND SCENERY, is respectfully submitted.

THE

Pictorial Sketch Book of Pennsylvania;

OR, ITS

SCENERY, INTERNAL IMPROVEMENTS,

RESOURCES, AND AGRICULTURE,

POPULARLY DESCRIBED BY ELI BOWEN,

AUTHOR OF "U. S. POST-OFFICE GUIDE," AND LATE OF THE GENERAL POST-OFFICE.

IN A HANDSOME OCTAVO VOLUME;

ILLUSTRATED WITH OVER TWO HUNDRED ENGRAVINGS,

AND CONTAINING

BARNES' COLORED MAP OF THE STATE,

THE LATEST AND BEST EXTANT.

Eighth Edition, Revised and Improved. Price only Two Dollars.

8,000 COPIES SOLD SINCE PUBLICATION.

The undersigned would respectfully invite the attention of the Citizens of Pennsylvania, and all others who wish a faithful Portraiture of the "Keystone State" to this Work. No section of her vast domain has escaped the Pen of the Author, but each in its turn is accurately and graphically described, while the Mineral Resources and Internal Improvements claim especial attention.

Persons, by remitting $2, will have a copy of the Work sent them free of expense.

Good Agents wanted in every County in the State. Address,

WM. WHITE SMITH, Publisher,
No. 195 Chestnut Street, Philadelphia.

PHILADELPHIA BOOK STORE.
R. H. SEE & CO.,
NO. 106 CHESTNUT STREET.

Publication Office of Graham's Magazine and the Saturday Evening Mail.

A COMPLETE ASSORTMENT OF

BOOKS, PERIODICALS, STATIONERY, PRINTS, &c.,

Which will be furnished for Cash at Publisher's prices. Postage prepaid, if ordered by Mail, to the residence of parties ordering.

GRAHAM'S MAGAZINE, FOR 1854,

Will be greatly enlarged and improved, and will contain, among other attractions, an

ILLUSTRATED LIFE OF WASHINGTON.
BY J. T. HEADLEY.

THE ILLUSTRATIONS

Will be done in the highest style of art, by the most competent Artists in New York and Philadelphia, and we look for a National response to this effort such as "Graham" has never had before.

Among the contributors to this volume, we are happy to announce Mrs. ANN S. STEPHENS, E. ANNA LEWIS, GRACE GREENWOOD, Mrs. JULIA C. R. DORR, WILLIAM CULLEN BRYANT, J. R. LOWELL, HENRY W. LONGFELLOW, E. P. WHIPPLE, JOHN G. SAXE, WILLIAM DOWE, and Dr. WM. ELDER, whose able articles will make "Graham" widely sought after and read.

It will be seen that "Graham" is in earnest for 1854 in his endeavors to keep the Magazine front in the rank of American Literary Monthlies—a position it has held for 27 years.

POSTAGE.—Subscribers in any part of the United States may now receive Graham's Magazine, by mail, at 3 cents a number, or 36 cents a year, payable at the Post-office where it is received.

TERMS.—The Terms of Graham's Magazine are Three Dollars for single subscribers. For Six Dollars in advance, one copy is sent three years. Two copies, one year, Five Dollars.

THE SATURDAY EVENING MAIL

Is a Weekly Family Paper, of a higher order than the usual run of journals of that character, and contains the best ORIGINAL STORIES, SELECTIONS FROM THE FOREIGN REVIEWS, MAGAZINES, AND JOURNALS, ORIGINAL ESSAYS UPON PUBLIC AFFAIRS, TEMPERANCE, SCIENCE, MUSIC, FASHION, and ART.

Specimen copies of the Saturday Evening Mail, and also of Graham's Magazine, will, at any time, be furnished *gratis* to strangers to the works, upon application as above, post-paid.

Milton Keynes UK
Ingram Content Group UK Ltd.
UKHW040701150224
437844UK00007B/706